W9-DEA-164

MORNING RADIO II:

Turning the Science Into Art

Tracy Johnson

WITHDRAWN

Published By:
Tracy Johnson
www.tjohnsonmedia.com

Printed By:
Books Just Books
www.booksjustbooks.com

MORNING RADIO II:

Turning the Science Into Art

Hundreds of Ideas to Help You Become a More Effective On-Air Superstar

By: Tracy Johnson

www.tjohnsonmedia.com

Ordering Information
To purchase additional copies, contact Tracy Johnson at www.tjohnsonmedia.com or email tjohnso1@san.rr.com. Quantity discounts are available.

ISBN   0-9714602-0-5

Library of Congress Catalog-in-Publication Data

Johnson, Tracy

Library of Congress Control Number: 2001119348

Published By:
Tracy Johnson

Printed By:
RJ Communications, Inc.

First Printing: 2001

MORNING RADIO II:

Turning the Science Into Art

Copyright 2001 Tracy D. Johnson. All rights reserved. No part of this publication may be reproduced, stored in a retrieval system or transmitted in any form or by any means electronic, mechanical, photocopying, recording or otherwise, without the prior written permission of the publisher.

ISBN 0-9714602-0-5

Library of Congress Control Number: 2001119348

Printed in the United States of America

I want to thank everyone who has helped me in the endless process of learning the dynamics of creating entertainment on the air and managing great air talent. There have been hundreds of influences that have helped me formulate my philosophies along the way and to all of you, I am much indebted.

"(The reader) will take from my book what he can bring to it. The dull witted will get dullness and the brilliant may find things in my book I didn't know were there."

-John Steinbeck, 1952

CONTENTS

PART 1: STUNTS

The mechanics, reasons and methods of creating attention through stunting.

PART 2: CONTESTS

Strategy and execution of games and interactive content to extend Time Spent Listening

PART 3: FEATURES

Ideas to create Benchmarks

PART 4: INTERVIEWS

Interacting with guests and celebrities on the air

PART 5: PROMOTING THE SHOW

Using all resources to create publicity

PART 6: MISCELLANEOUS

Thoughts on other important matters

PART 7: HOLIDAYS
A comprehensive promotion guide

PART 8: SHOW PREP

Thought-Starters for Each Month

INTRODUCTION
THE MISSION OF *MORNING RADIO II*

In *Morning Radio*, Alan Burns and I outlined the principles and guidelines of what it takes to become more than just a successful air talent, but a dominant and potentially legendary air personality. Out of the hundreds of positive comments and reviews we received, the most gratifying feedback was this email:

Dear Tracy,

> "I have just finished reading your book *Morning Radio* for the third time, and all I have to say is, "Duhhhh....it's all common sense."

Great personality radio is *common sense*. It's *simple*. But it's *not* easy. *Morning Radio* provided an outline of the basics for a personality-oriented show to come alive. It's a textbook that offers a basic starting point. But just as a recipe needs a great chef to create a culinary masterpiece, even the best guidance requires an expert practitioner to create a compelling show.

Morning Radio II takes the principles and concepts in *Morning Radio* and applies them. There are hundreds of ideas to help you identify particular elements that can be adapted to enhance your character and help you become a more compelling air personality.

In all of radio, there are only a few *great* bits that work on their own, and not that many *good* ones. Even then, the great ideas are not so powerful that they can overcome average execution. Many years ago, the Who sang "It's the singer, not the song....that makes you sing along". In morning radio, it's the personality that creates great radio segments resulting in interest and passion with your audience.

This collection of applications and ideas is a great place to start. But it is only the beginning. The book *"Morning Radio For Dummies"* doesn't exist, but probably should. Maybe that will be the title for *Morning Radio III.* There is no correspondence course that you can take and instantly achieve celebrity success on the air. The fact is that there are no simple steps to insure stardom. It takes commitment, hard work, intelligence and determination. It's what you *do* with an idea that can turn you into a million dollar morning show.

Real: Actual, authentic, genuine, sincere, bona fide, actual. In short, it's the process of being natural and original!

Most morning shows strive to be *"real"*. That's a buzzword in our business. But in the process of being "real", they fail to be riveting or compelling. The pursuit of "real" has eliminated most of the entertainment. The result is lackluster, boring radio shows. Being real is often used as an excuse for lack of proper preparation. Who is real? Seinfeld? Drew Carey? They're great performers, but all work from a carefully crafted script prepared by a team of writers. The magic of being "real on the air" is creating an on-air character that is based on the real-life character of the personalities. Without proper preparation, brainstorming and execution, great ideas are wasted.

So, why do so many morning shows miss "the point"?

See *Morning Radio* Chapter 5

Mostly, it's a result of not understanding the audience, the station or even their own personality. Often, personalities don't know enough about their listener, their station, or their images in the market to prepare an effective show. Many times, the PD has failed to communicate the mission to the talent. That's a problem, but it is not an acceptable excuse. You, as an air talent, must accept the responsibility to tap into the "vibe" in your market, and understand your listeners.

Motivation: Stimulus, incentive, inspiration, driving force. Motivation is the reason for doing what you do!

Detroit Lions defensive coordinator Jerry Sullivan coaches his players with a philosophy that programmers should adopt for their air talent. He believes you can't expect a player to execute an assignment unless the player really understands exactly *why* he's supposed to do it a particular way. He is always *teaching* his players and not just ordering them around. That's real coaching! And it produces real results.

Perhaps a more common problem is that the show has lost sight of who they are and how they fit into their listener's world. Self-awareness of the show is not only critical to reaching the next level; it's an integral survival skill in an increasingly competitive arena. Maybe the show is falling into a rut, or just lacking *motivation*, which leads to passive shows, and passive audience response.

In this book, you will learn how to apply principles presented in *Morning Radio*, along with the reasons *why* they work and complete explanations of the thought process behind those ideas to make your on-air performance come alive every day! *Morning Radio II* is a simple, straightforward explanation of how to increase creativity on the radio.

Morning Radio II not only offers new ideas, but also demonstrates what makes these ideas successful on the air. You'll find real examples of stations and personalities that have used these tactics bring the concepts to life. You'll find out how to implement new contests, ideas, topics and stunts to engage and entertain listeners and increase your presence as a high profile on-air personality.

Each section contains everything you need to execute great ideas, from conception of the idea to celebration of the event. Not only will you learn *what* to do, you'll find out *who* should do them, *why* they work, and *when* they should be done. It's a textbook for success. By studying the examples, you'll begin to understand the *process* of creating memorable radio, and that understanding will lead to thousands of ideas that will work on *your* show.

There is no doubt that you've heard of many of the ideas before. Perhaps you've even used these ideas on your station. The goal of this book is not to simply provide ideas to slap on your show immediately. It's to make you think through the reasons why specific bits work or don't, and to appreciate and enjoy the process of creating great radio.

As in most aspects of society, the radio industry tends to

Most broadcasters over-react to Arbitron. Radio stations should be treated like product brands. If Colgate toothpaste has a weak sales quarter, they don't change the product. But radio stations have a "down" ratings period, and many managers press the panic button. They want to change the music, or the talent, or the fomat! Remember, Arbitron is only estimates.

reward the *results* of effort more than the effort itself. In the short term, that thinking may produce Arbitron success. But if you focus exclusively on results, eventually your creativity will be reduced, innovation stifled and your standards will be lowered. In this book, I hope to help you achieve better results through a more detailed dedication to the *process* of creating great moments on the air.

Former UCLA basketball coach John Wooden understood the importance of keeping his teams focused on the present, in order to avoid the far-off rewards of upcoming games and seasons. Wooden refused to use the terms "winning" or "beat" with his teams. To him, victory was the result of his team executing their plan and "outscoring the competition". This helped keep his teams focused on executing the basics with a dedication to excellence. Taking pride in the process produced unmatched results. When you focus on your performance rather than the prize, you increase your chances for success.

In radio, I have learned that if you dedicate your efforts to creating great moments on the air, with a commitment to appealing to your audience's emotions, positive ratings will follow. Ratings rewards are rarely "on time". If your measures of success are attached to the next ratings period, you'll be
disappointed more often than not, and your career will stall as you constantly tinker with your show and performance out of frustration in not receiving the validation of the ratings reward.

If you're a programmer, this book can make you a hero with

your talent. If you are talent, a producer or work on a morning
show in any capacity, it will give you inspiration and direction to help connect with your listeners daily!

Packed with examples and detailed guidance, I hope *Morning Radio II* will become just as valuable to you as *Morning Radio.*

Tracy Johnson

Part One: Stunts
The Mechanics, Reasons and Methods of Creating Attention through Stunting

-1-

Why Do Stunts?

Stunts are perhaps *the* easiest, fastest and best method of creating tremendous word-of-mouth with you listeners and capturing free media attention in your market. From the "What Would You Do" contests to charity-related events, many stations and shows have used outrageous attention-getting events to help establish their familiarity.

As with most things in radio, there are few truly unique, new and different ideas. Most morning shows will have successful results by *duplicating or re-working something that has already been done.* It's silly to dismiss an idea simply because you know a show in another market beat you to it. They probably stole it from someone else! Take ideas, input and inspiration from any source you can, and use them to your advantage.

Daypart: A time window, as defined by the ratings services. The five Arbitron dayparts are morning drive (6-10am), midday (10a-3pm), after-noon drive (3-7pm), evening (7pm-12m) and over-night (12m-6am).

As the key *daypart* on most stations, the morning show is the stage for most outrageous and highest-profile events. Well-executed stunts will create talk about the show ("did you hear what they did this morning?") and more importantly, generate media attention.

Use stunts to gain attention for the show, but don't let them become the primary reason to listen to the show.

They can, and often do, become habit forming. Many shows began a downward spiral because they spent too much time dreaming up outrageous ways to shock their audience instead of focusing on how to entertain them. In other words, stunts are a form of marketing the show, not the show itself. It's very important to understand the difference. Don't become so dependent on events and then wonder why the show lacks the impact it once had.

Remember that stunts are like a special weekend sale at a retail outlet. For a few days, sales skyrocket and the store is packed with eager customers. But when prices return to normal, business returns to normal and the benefit from the advertising campaign expires. That doesn't mean weekend sales are ineffective. The point is that a retail outlet relying too heavily on sales will end up with customers who only shop when their merchandise is reduced. If you rely too heavily on outrageous stunts to drive listeners to your show, you'll never break free of the pressure to come up with something to "top" your past feats.   If you develop a valid personality for your show, and understand how stunts fit into your program and marketing mix, then apply them properly, they can be a powerful tool.

The best stunts are usually a result of knowing what ideas to borrow and creatively applying those ideas to your circumstances

-2-

WHEN TO DO STUNTS?

I f you have an impressivestunt for a new show, wait until the show sounds great before executing the stunt. Successful acts will yield a cume increase, especially if it catches the attention of local television stations. If the show itself isn't developed to the point that it can attract and hold listeners yet, the end result will do more damage than the short-term gain. A new business would not hold a grand opening until the store is 100% ready. Neither should your show employ such a powerful weapon that will attract new listeners until it is fully up-to-speed.

Product Life Cycle: The natural ebb and flow of any product's introduction, acceptance, growth and decline.

So it's important to evaluate your show and identify where it is in development. The Randy Lane Company equates this process to a business identifying where it is in the *product life cycle*. When you determine where you are in your life cycle, it's easier to see how stunts might fit into your show:

1. **Introduction.** You're new to the market. In this phase, stunts can be used to gain attention and make a statement that you have arrived. Stunts should be consistent with your overall personality in this phase, but the most important consideration is whether or not your stunt will attract attention and facilitate audience retention

of your name and call letters. You can take a few more risks in the introduction phase, since your image has not yet been entrenched and early mistakes can be overcome more easily.

2. **New/Growing with limited awareness**. Here, you've been introduced, and you're using stunts to begin developing your character and personality. Gaining attention and creating talk is still important, but now you are more concerned about the nature, values and personality you wish to project.

3. **Mature.** Your show is hot and on-the-rise. Stunts must be very carefully considered here. You're on your way to the top, but not there yet. This is where poorly considered stunts can backfire. Think *everything* through. Be more concerned about your image and how any particular stunt can enhance it.

4. **Peak A** (recently exceeded highest market expectations). This is actually a part of the "mature" phase in the product life cycle. In this phase, stunts are probably not needed as frequently. This is the time many shows introduce new characters to become the risk-takers, while the main personalities on the show act as "ring-master". At this time, performing fewer stunts will pay higher dividends, and should be used to extend this phase as long as possible.

5. **Peak B** (has been at the top over time). This is the second part of the maturity phase in the show's life cycle. It's the uncomfortable period of time where *apathy* begins to set in, with the show and with the audience. By this time, you've worked for years to become a part of your listener's lifestyle, and now you've become so comfortable that they begin taking you for granted. If you have avoided major stunts for a period of time (in the Peak A phase), this is the time to rework old ideas or create fresh new stunts to inject new life and excitement into the show. If you can re-package and re-vitalize the show, you could even return the show to the Peak A phase.

6. **Decline.** Competition starts to eat away at shares, audiences become less impressed, or worse, disinterested in the show, and no matter what you try on the air, it seems to fall flat. Listeners start to get the feeling that the show is "out of touch". At this point, it's probably too late for stunts to rescue the show. You need to overhaul everything and get back to basics, so stunts have limited value.

7. **Never got off the ground**. Though not charted on most product life cycle graphs, too many shows fall into this category and never move. Many shows fail to become a "hit" because they fail to properly identify where they are in the

Apathy: Indifference, lack of concern, lethargy, boredom, indifference, laziness. A basic character trait of many air personalities product cycle. They may execute a great idea perfectly, but it is inappropriate for the show and therefore, fails. These shows continue to struggle, and search for their position, but never quite get over the hump.

Stunts often become habit-forming. When a successful stunt brings attention to your show, it's enticing to follow it up with another. Be aware that if you perform many stunts, eventually you will achieve "category dominance" for an image you may not want!

It sounds cliché, but it's worth saying. If a stunt is worth doing at all, it's worth doing right. Enlist the cooperation of the promotions department (setup, publicity and media alerts) and all other dayparts (cross promotion) in helping publicize the stunt and build the event into something even more meaningful.

-3-

STUNTS NEED A TRIGGER!

The most important advice I could offer anyone considering stunts as a major part of the show is to always have a reason for the stunt. The reason is the "trigger". Stunts that fail are usually because the audience doesn't see any reason for the stunt to take place. If you think about it, you'll be able to identify dozens of examples of shows that perform something outrageous merely for the shock value. These stunts may get some attention, but fail to produce lasting images.

In 1993, Jeff & Jer took advantage of the bungee jumping craze by having Jeff perform a bungee jump live on the air. It was topical, but it became significant to the listeners because of the way the bit was introduced. It started with a "what are you afraid of" segment on the show, during which Jeff revealed on the air that he had an intense fear of heights. This fear became the "trigger" that developed into Jeff facing and overcoming his personal fear (character development) by performing the bungee-jump (topicality). With the encouragement of the rest of the show, and hundreds of listeners, Jeff was successful in his jump. Listeners still talk about it to this day. By personalizing his fear, Jeff & Jer elevated the stunt to a level that created a passionate and emotional moment on the air. Listeners were crying with happiness and pride because they were

Stunts work because listeners have proven over and over that they will respond to shows that "get away with things I could never do". It's a way for listeners to experience adventure without risk..

able to identify with Jeff. Creating that *emotional bond* with listeners is one of the essential keys to becoming meaningful celebrities in your market.

The best stunts are the result of a taking advantage of a topic that is already top-of-mind to the audience. These stunts usually happen spontaneously and opportunistic personalities brainstorm the idea until it begins to take on a life of it's own. Brainstorming session should be held regularly to address hot topics!

Emotional bond: A powerful connection that links the personality with the audience in a way that transcends anything tangible

One of the best attention-getting events ever staged was a spontaneous idea that happened in Pittsburgh in 1989. Pittsburgh Pirates radio announcer, and former major leaguepitcher Jim Rooker was the color analyst with a penchant for his humor and candor in describing Pirates games. The Pirates were playing the last game of a long, losing road trip in Philadelphia. In the first inning, the Pirates took a 10-0 lead, when Rooker commented, "It's been a bad road trip, but if you are going to win just one game, it might as well be the last one. In fact, if we lose this game, I'll walk home." Well, anything can happen in baseball, and on that night it did! The Phillies rallied and won the game, 15-11.

The next morning, Rooker started at home plate and began a 13-day, 320 mile walk to make good on his promise. When he arrived in Pittsburgh, both sides of the street were packed, and he had raised $81,000 for charity. Rooker commented, "Thank God we weren't playing San Francisco." If Rooker, the air personality, had participated in a typical walk-a-thon, the event wouldn't have created news coverage. This walk, however, captured the public's attention because it was inspired by a current event that had a natural, if unexpected, "trigger".

Sports have provided the "trigger" for many stunts that have become legendary for the personalities that executed them. Chicago radio listeners and sports fans will never forget the July 12, 1979 "Disco Demolition" promotion that elevated Steve Dahl to the status of market celebrity at WLUP/Chicago. Between games of a White Sox/Indians doubleheader, Dahl blew up a pile of listener-contributed disco records. The frenzy that ensued was so extreme that the second game was cancelled and the White Sox had to forfeit. Dahl's promotion was boldly hosted by one of history's most high profile promoters, White

Sox owner Bill Veeck. The "horror at Comiskey" as a Chicago newspaper called it, was described by Dahl, "It looks like World War II out here." Dahl's sense of timing was perfect! He knew that his audience (a rock station) always *hated* disco, and he also calculated that the disco fad was waning. His place in history transcended that of mere air personality, and is credited with single-handedly "killing disco" with this stunt!

Mancow Muller was well on his way to becoming a nationally known personality already, but his profile was greatly enhanced when he mimicked Bill Clinton's haircut

It's easy to perform a stunt! It's not so easy to create a public event that connects with your audience's emotions. Feelings grab your listener and make them feel connected. The measure of a successful stunt is not how much media you generate, but how successful you are in creating a lasting impression!

aboard Air Force I by having his own "haircut" in a car on the San Francisco Bay Bridge that tied up traffic for hours and turned the city upside down. Not only was it controversial, he incurred the wrath – and attention – of an entire market for several weeks.

On the other hand, stunts without a natural "launch" fall flat. They come up short of their potential if they are only staged for their shock value. I once worked with a very talented show that had an idea to have their sports reporter perform his report in a public locaation---*in the nude*. In a planning session, I asked "why"? The answer, "He's willing to do it, and everyone will talk about it." After lengthy debate, they went through with it. The show went on the air and simply said, "Our crazy sports guy is going to do the sports naked next Friday morning in public".

The results:

1. Listeners thought the crazy sports guy was just weird. Not clever, not daring, not outrageous, not fun. Just strange.

2. Only about 20 people came to the event.

3. No press or media covered the event. There was no *reason* to cover it (the show never gave them a good reason, and we didn't promote the event to the media properly). There was no storyline attached. What would the media have said about it in their coverage?

> Brainstorm: Think, dream up, create, come up with, an original idea. The strength behind many shows is the ability to brainstorm ordinary ideas into something extraordinary

How to promote your show to the media is covered in Part 5

The stunt was a great idea, and had the potential to be a memorable event, but was missing a *reason*. It would have been even better if he had been arrested and spent a night in jail! It could have worked if they had taken the time to *brainstorm*, create risk, and use the stunt as a payoff for a bet that was lost or (like the Jim Rooker example), the follow through of a promise if an unlikely event occurred.

Something as simple as paying off a bet for the men in a month-long Battle Of The Sexes contest would have worked. The personality would have been better remembered if he or she had paid off the bit reluctantly rather than being so willing to strip down to do the sportscast. In this case, *poor planning, set-up and development dulled a great idea.*

Before embarking on a stunt, first ask yourself, "why?", then ask "how will we measure success?"

-4-

Stunts Develop Character

S tunts are great for character development of your show, and the individual personalities on the show. Similarly, many stunts fall flat because the activity is out of character for the personality involved. It's important to understand that just as there are many different styles or characters, there are many different types of stunts that can be staged.

If you strive to develop a personality profile that is outrageous, spontaneous, and create a "I can't believe what they did" image, stunts are perfect for you. On the other hand, if you are building a character of being the friendly, warm and fuzzy show, a very different approach to stunt development is required. Remember that the type of stunt should not only match your morning show personality, but fit into the image your station is trying to develop as well.

To illustrate, let's take a simple promotional topic, and develop several examples of stunts that various types of morning shows could be effective in staging.

The idea is a Holiday Toy Drive for a local charity. The station goal is to gather as many toys as possible for underprivileged children. Obviously, this is a popular campaign that most stations and shows have participated in

Building character on your show: *Morning Radio I*, **Chapter 6**

at some point. The typical approach to this promotion is to tug on the heartstrings of listeners, playing on their sympathy to make the holiday season brighter for those less fortunate. However, with a little creativity, you can turn this into a dynamic, exciting event that creates compelling radio, local media coverage and a memorable point of reference for years to come. Here are three approaches:

1. The morning show is a "good neighbor" type show that relies on creating warm and fuzzy feelings and promotes family values, holiday traditions, etc. This show focuses on the memories of the show members from when they were growing up, and what it was that they wanted (but didn't get) for Christmas. A member of the show relates that their family went through hard times and when they were 10, all they wanted was a bicycle, describing the bike in *detail.* Their heart was broken when mom and dad finally had to explain that they didn't have the money for the bike. You may have to create this story, but that's okay-this is theater, remember? Phone calls flood in from listeners with similar memories, and the holiday toy drive becomes a *bike* drive, so no kid in your community has to go through the same thing. The campaign culminates in a one-day event at a public location where listeners bring bicycles, or cash to purchase bicycles.

2. The morning show is an outrageous, rebel type show that is always straddling the line of good taste and barely staying out of trouble. They are always living on the edge. This type of show does things

their listeners *wish* they could get away with. Their approach is to set up a Santa Claus at a mall to collect toys for the toy drive (they promote it but to this point it's not a station promotion). After a week or so, the show crashes the mall, kidnaps the Santa Claus at gunpoint, and holds him hostage. Santa won't be released until the goal of xxx toys is donated to the mall. Threats are made several times a day, with the show calling in from the secret location where Santa is being held in captivity. When the goal is reached (4-6 days later), Santa is returned, unharmed. Albie Dee (WXYV/Baltimore) staged this stunt a few years ago.

3. The show is a playful, fun, "never know what will happen next" type show. They are always doing things that are a little off-center and outrageous to create talk. This show could take on the promotion by accepting personal risk and involving the listener vicariously through their experiences until a goal is reached is their method. Sitting on a billboard in the freezing cold, being buried in a mountain of snow, or being "buried alive" in a block of ice provide dramatic settings for live, marathon broadcasts to increase sympathy and awareness for the cause.

Stunts are also effective when they engage the listener's fantasy. A few years ago, Jeff & Jer conducted "Fantasy Week". Each day, they promised to fulfill a listener's fantasy. One of the most memorable featured an all-out food fight in a parking lot. Armed with a fully catered, five course buffet of nearly every kind of messy food imaginable, the entire show engaged the listener and 10 of her friends in a food fight that would have made Hollywood proud.

Stunts require a talent that is able to take a simple idea and create multiple angles within that simple story "arc". (see story-telling in Part 6: Miscellaneous)

Prepare for success! Only perform stunts that you will be proud of when you reach your ultimate goals in the market. In other words, design your stunts to fulfill and support your desired future image, rather than your current image. Stunts may yield short term benefits, but they have long-term impact.

From The Desk Of...Erich Fromm

Character is essentially formed by a person's experiences, especially of those in early life, and changeable, to some extent, by insights and new kinds of experiences

-Erich Fromm, psychiatrist

-5-

ARE STUNTS RIGHT FOR YOU?

D o you *need* to do stunts in order to be successful? Of course not! Some of the most successful, high profile personalities of all time have completely avoided, or at least not relied heavily on, stunting. You may be able to recall an occasional event that Rick Dees and Scott Shannon have staged, but most performers understand that their ultimate success rests on their ability to connect to an audience, not simply shocking them.

Some shows simply should not do stunts, but as long as they are performed at the right time and for the right reasons, most shows are able to do them at some level. With the proper brainstorming, presentation and staging, stunts can be a powerful weapon in gaining publicity and attention.

Stunts are generally very difficult to execute to perfection. To maximize the impact, personalities must be great storytellers, with a flair for the theatrical. For maximum impact, stunts require an ability to build the event (hype) to capture the imagination of the listening public. It takes a special personality to be able to paint a picture with words that are descriptive, creative and spark the imagination of

If the stunt isn't working, have a plan to bail out gracefully!

the casual listener.

Some shows shouldn't attempt stunts because the audience would not accept it as part of the expectation for the station or the show. Many R&B stations avoid stunting. In an article in Airplay Monitor magazine (June 15, 2001), Radio One/Superadio syndicataed morning host Russ Parr explained, "Stunts don't work in urban radio, because (the audience) think it's corny. It's the same reason you don't see us bungee jumping or on those (reality) TV shows where a guy is getting beat up by a deer." KPRS/Kansas City PD Sam Weaver agrees, "Stunting doesn't work on R&B radio, because it doesn't fit the image. Most stations are primarily targeting females, and stunts don't get over with them. That's why you don't see this on AC stations either." Parr continues, "we have to be careful because black folks hold you more accountable in terms of setting a moral tone. They will call you out if (they feel you're) crossing the line."

There are also regional differences that make some stunts work in one market, but be considered too aggressive in others. What is tolerated, or perhaps barely even noticed, in New York City may cause a public outrage in Boise. Personalities and programmers must be conscious of what is legal, moral *and* ethical, as defined by their community standards in the markets they serve.

Even with flawless execution, many great ideas have been ruined because the personalities involved simply couldn't make the stunt come alive to their listeners.

-6-

WHEN STUNTS BACKFIRE

You've undoubtedly heard the phrase "there's no such thing as bad publicity", or "all press is good press, as long as they spell the name right". There is merit in these statements, but is it *true* in every case? After all, your goal is to get coverage on local TV and newspapers.

As air talent continues to be more *outrageous* than past stunts, listeners and local public officials have become outraged, and in some cases have even brought about legal action. Does this notoriety help a station or inflict damage? After all is said and done, has the media coverage helped or hurt Monica Lewinsky? Vanilla Ice? Eminem? Short term notoriety does not automatically translate into long-term success.

Outrageous: The literal definition of this term is shameful, disgraceful, shocking, contemptible, extreme and offensive. Are you sure you want to describe your personality as "outrageous"?

DC101/Washington DC personality Elliot Segal encouraged listeners to get a photograph kissing Yasser Arafat during an official White House visit, which resulted in a permanent record with the Secret Service. Bubba The Love Sponge became the center of controversy when he killed a wild boar in the parking lot of WXTB in Tampa. Animal rights groups even went so far as to press charges for animal cruelty. Willie B's Chicken Drop and Dick Dale's "Spank the Monkey" contest are other recent examples of stunts that may have crossed the line of good taste.

In an interview with FMQB Magazine, Clear Channel Director of FM Programming/Denver Mike O'Conner said, "If you put the community good will at risk, a stunt is over-the-edge. In this day and age, over-the-edge is also when the financial liability is greater than the reward, which is usually most."

Paragon Research conducted a project to address the impact of such stunts on a station's ratings and found that listeners will go out of their way to under-report listening to a station that performs a stunt that they feel is in bad taste. That brings you to the all-important question: "When negative publicity hits your show or station for a stunt, how is it perceived by your *audience*? Your actual listeners may have a much different impression than the special interest groups or publicity seekers that criticize your activities. KBPI/Denver's morning show (Dean & Rog) created a stir when they reacted to a story that Moslems refuse to salute the American flag. They sent an intern out to play the National Anthem in a mosque during services. The negative press was predictable, but the station got a clear ratings boost out of it. Why? Their audience, and potential KBPI listeners had a very different response than the public that was offended.

Character: An individual, or creature, that may or may not be based on reality. A character fills a role that adds personality and dimension to the show.

Many times, the value of a controversial stunt must be balanced against the economic pain that may result. You may benefit from a short-term ratings gain, but when advertisers cancel management won't be pleased. Staying within the acceptance of the community's standards is the key. When you cross your market's line of "good taste" you've gone too far, and earning back that trust is more difficult than gaining it in the first place.

When, or if, something goes wrong, don't point fingers to mitigate the blame. Take responsibility, and plan for avoiding the same mistake next time! Those who don't learn from their past will repeat it. Those who repeat their mistakes should find another line of work.

Stunt Mission

In Marie Claire magazine, Susan Sarandon went on a mission very much like a radio stunt boy. Here are a few of the missions that she had to complete:

1-Take a bite out of a strangers sandwich.
2-Wash a man's hair.
3-Convince a man to dye his hair blonde.
4-Finagle a free pastry from a bakery
5-Ask a man to dance with you in the street.
6-Ask a man to buy his girlfriend a flower.
7-Ask to try on a man's uniform.
8-Get in a photo with a bride and a groom.
9-Organize a "Hands Across Wall Street."
10-Get a businessman to take off his tie

STUNTS: MAJOR OR MINOR?

E very stunt doesn't have to be a major stunt. Many stations create a character whose specialty is being a stunt guy (calling pizzas, elevator bits, etc). This allows the personalities to be the "ring-master, not the circus act", and it provides the opportunity to capture the "you'll never know what they're going to do next" image. It is essential, however to create drama and risk in the stunt.

A few years ago, 99X/Atlanta created controversy, and shocking risk when Leslie Framm lost a bet, and the payoff was for her to have her pinky finger cut off. The show took you right to the edge (and many would argue it went right over the edge), complete with sound effects of a power saw. The beauty of the bit was that it created such powerful emotion in the audience and built character for Leslie's personality. Did it really happen? Did they go through with it? I wouldn't want to spoil it for you, or their listeners. You see, drama, and the uncertainty of the reality, is part of the intrigue that makes it work.

Having a "Danger Boy" on your show can create moments that pull listeners into the show emotionally as they experience minor stunts through the experience of the *character.* Simple things like having Danger Boy in a public area making odd announcements with a megaphone and

More Stunt Boy ideas at tjohnsonmedia.com

capturing the responses of unsuspecting passers-by are priceless.

K102/Minneapolis had a character named "Captain Intersection", who dressed in a ridiculous outfit and goes to a different area of the city. He then gives clues on the air, and when listeners find him, they pick up prizes.

The key to making a character effective as a "stunt boy" is to do them frequently, regularly, creatively and topically. Avoid doing them "just to do them".

Major stunts are difficult to pull off. It's the attention to detail that makes all the difference. Never let anything interfere with your chances of success. Jeff & Jer's producer at Star 100.7/San Diego is "Little" Tommy Sablan. In addition to his obvious abilities, the real secret to Tommy's success is his persistence and dedication to success. Nothing, absolutely nothing, is too big an obstacle for Tommy to overcome!

8

IDEAS FOR STUNT BOY

If you have a Stunt Boy, or Danger Boy, or Street Turd, or any of the dozens of clever names the low man on the ladder gets on the show, use them frequently! It's funny to hear the hapless victim tied with duct tape, stuffed in a garbage can and rolled down a bumpy hill! If you don't mind making your Stunt Boy look stupid (and why would you have one if your main goal is to protect their image?), here are some examples of ideas that could lead to on-air magic. This, of course is not a comprehensive list, but should serve as a thought-starter.

- Call a 7-11, tell them you can see them on the internet. Describe what they are doing in detail. Your stunt boy is out in front of the store telling you what is going on inside.

- Handcuff you stunt boy to a telephone booth, with the keys a few feet away from him. He has to convince someone to hand him the key.

- Dress up like an inmate, with the jumpsuit, handcuffs and leg shackles. Go into a hardware store and ask to borrow a saw. Watch out, though! KYLD/San Francisco personalities ended up receiving a fine, jail time and a fine for doing this

See *Morning Radio 1*, Chapter 8

one!

- Try and negotiate with "street people"

- Live in a jail cell for a week

- Dress up as a woman, and send him to a gynecologist

- Go into Starbucks and tell them you've never had coffee before and would like to try a double espresso. Take one sip and go berserk. "Yee-Haw...Who's Your Daddy...remember the Alamo." Jump up on the counter and start beating your chest, grab the paper out of some guys hands and yell "Buy a car with no money down!!!"

Creating drama gives you the power to tap into a listener's imagination. Handled carelessly, you will be perceived as contrived and unbelievable. Handle with care!

-9-

GREAT STUNTS YOU CAN DO

Doing big stunts are fun. They create attention, and will get you on the six o'clock news. If you're going to do a big stunt, do it *really* big. Don't just hold a food drive. Suspend your entire show from a crane 500 feet in the air until 100,000 pounds of food is raised. Or how about having your show live as homeless people on the streets of your city until the goal is reached. Or maybe you could camp out in a tent at a parking lot or football field until the entire area is covered completely with donated food. Think big. Think creatively. And think visually.

Before you consider stunts as a major part of your show's focus, first make sure it fits into your show's Mission Statement. Then, make sure it fits your character role. Finally, match the stunt to your on-air personality, and make sure the stunt is performed with the proper setup.

Many radio stations and morning shows have staged variations of the "what's the craziest thing you would do" stunt, where listeners compete for a prize by performing outrageous and disgusting acts. It almost always gets noticed, usually gets press, but routinely fails to produce lasting benefits. Usually, listeners are left with the impression that "radio listeners are weird and that radio personality is juvenile." There are better ways to capture the public's attention, and create powerful media coverage.

Each stunt should be carefully crafted to create drama in the story. Sure you can get *contest pigs* to do the most unimaginable act in public for hard-to-get tickets, but unless you develop a story line, and put the contest into context, it will sound stupid.

Contest Pig: An affectionate term for your most ardent, loyal listeners

It is essential to develop drama and a sense of anticipation for the climactic event. Develop character and imagination as the bit develops. Remember the five-steps to creating great bits-the hook, set up, dress up, payoff and black out.

In all stunts, remember to plan the payoff with the listener's schedule in mind. They have short attention spans. Don't expect them to sit through long set ups unless you do a great job in hooking them into the bit. Generally, the stronger the idea, the longer you can ride it. But in an age of listeners demanding instant gratification, you must be aware of the importance of getting to the point quickly!

Here are some thought starters for some great stunts that can attract attention for your station and your show. Remember, each of these is an *idea* that can be modified, adapted and crafted for various situations.

-10-

"Live in it to Win it"

This promotion has been around since the mid-80s, and is one of the most interesting methods ever designed to give away a car. Four contestants enter a car. The last one living in the car wins it.

This promotion can easily be adapted to other large-ticket items (camper, trailer, condo, etc). The concept is very simple, and rules are not complex. Contestants live in the car 24/7. They get a pre-determined number (3-6) of short (10-15 minute) breaks per day. During the breaks, they can do anything they want as long as they are back in the car on time. Plus, anything that comes into the car must stay in the car throughout the contest (including food, wrappers, etc). Their only form of entertainment is your station. No books, no magazines, etc.

How To Do It:

Be sure to have a microphone in the car at all times, so you can eavesdrop on the conversation at any time. Maintain a live "presence" at the site at all times. Enforce the rules of the contest.

When To Do It:

Anytime is fine. Timing usually is dependent on your auto

dealer partner. They will likely require it to be held in their showroom in order to generate traffic for their dealership, but if you can persuade them to hold it at a more public location, it works better.

Pros:

Great media. Great theatre on the air. You create a story line that is exciting for the audience to follow. Executed properly, you will create "can't miss" moments on the air.

Cons:

The contest requires frequent promotion, and more importantly, terrific "story telling" ability from your talent. As the contest continues from day-to-day and week-to-week, it becomes more challenging to create fresh angles to the story. After someone drops out, it works to bring local (and national) celebrities out to take their place for periods of time. Also, have your personalities join in the contest. To keep the contest moving forward, and insure an "end date", you may want to have listeners "vote contestants out" at regular intervals.

Watch Out For:

Many shows (and stations) become bored with the contest after a week or two, but that's just when the audience is getting interested. It's essential to continue re-telling the story in new, creative ways. Be sure to have a plan in the event a natural winner doesn't happen. One way to do this is announce that each contestant must raise donations for

"Story Telling" is covered in detail in Part 6 of *Morning Radio II*

the station's chosen charity, and they have a specific period of time to generate those donations. Whoever raises the most wins the car, the runner-ups are awarded a lease of the same car.

Why It Works:

Hook: the ability to create a quick first impression engaging the listener's imagination to want to hear more.

One of the keys to developing great radio theater is creating moments on the air that create anticipation. The entertainment is in the way the car is given away, not the prize itself. After soliciting your contestants, focus all your promos and air time on the competition between the contestants and their personalities. The prize is important, but secondary. It's the *"hook"* to get contestants and listeners interested. It simply serves as the "why" they are doing this.

1. Interesting contestants. Choose people who have a personality that will attract listener participation. Nothing kills this contest faster than *boring* contestants.

2. *Endearinig* personalities. You MUST develop the personalities of the contestants so your listeners feel they "know" them. This is the responsibility of the programmer and air staff. The audience must feel a connection to the contestants so they feel as if they are involved in the event themselves-almost living vicariously through the contestants. The TV show "Survivor" exploited this concept exceptionally well, and this stunt provides the perfect vehicle

Endearing: Appealing, attractive, charming, engaging, winning.

for your station to do it, too.

3. Encourage (stage) competition between the contestants. Remember, controversy creates compelling entertainment. It also allows you the opportunity to put them through various challenges as part of the stunt (set up an annoying karaoke singer outside the car to sing for several hours, etc).

4. Create dramatic moments. Look for opportunities to develop sub-plots to the story regularly. Watch for subtle conflicts between contestants. Find details in their personal lives that you can exploit on the air between the major high points of the contest.

5. Stay interested. The talent will tire of this contest long before the audience does. It can be fatiguing to re-tell the story, but repeating the message is essential in building listener "equity" in the contest. Remember, they aren't paying attention as much as we would like them to!

Who Should Do It:

Shows that have, or wish to have, an "outrageous" or "fun" image. If it has never been done in your market, you should do it! If it's been five years or more since it's been done in your market, you should consider it.

Who Has Done It Before:

Dozens of stations have used this effectively. I first became aware of it in the mid-80s when Dave Shakes was PD at B96 in Chicago. Shakes generated tremendous media attention and captured the imagination of the radio industry with a terrific idea. Over the years, many variations have emerged. In fact, many stations modified the concept for their own Survivor-type contest when that television show reached maximum popularity.

Use a compact car to make it a little more difficult. Have a webcam placed inside the vehicle so listeners can watch everything on your website, participate in live chats and/or message boards with the contestants and/or vote on who should be kicked out of the contest

Live In it To Win It is a powerful promotion if you _commit to it!_ Sadly, commitment is a trait that is disappearing in radio. A deep belief in an idea, concept, program, format or personality is essential for success.

-11-

How Far Will You Go?

This stunt is relatively easy to do, and many stations have done a varaiation of it. The only essential requirement is that the prize be truly in demand. If you can obtain a big prize (not necessarily expensive, but difficult to obtain like Super Bowl Tickets, Backstage meeting with *major* artist, etc.) you have the incentive to try this. Listeners then submit their entries for what they would do to win that prize. The show reduces the list to a manageable level (5-10 at most). The contestants then must perform their act, and listeners or a panel of judges (celebrities?) vote for the winner.

Major: Main, key, foremost, most important. There can be only *one* "major".

When To Do It:

Anytime you have something that is *truly* in demand. The bigger the prize, and more difficult to obtain prize, the better. Even if you've done it before, "How Far Will You Go" or "What Would You Do" can be performed over and over. Some shows may even want to make this a regular event, performing quarterly or semi-annually.

Pros:

Great media coverage is virtually guaranteed. However, it's difficult to secure much more than the end-of-newscast "kicker story" on most television stations. It also makes for good phone action for a week or so while you qualify listeners to compete.

Cons:

Be sure the prize is difficult to obtain, and desirable, for a listener. By nature, this like a carnival sideshow. You'll get press, but it may not position your show properly with the audience that sees it. Sure, you can gross them out and make them talk, but be sure this is a good th*ing*.

Watch **Out For:**

Many of the entries you receive will be similar. Be sure to only accept a variety of acts. Don't let your event be a contest of who will eat the grossest things. Be creative! It's a nice touch to have a "surprise" consolation prize for the acts that don't win. For example, if you're giving away a meeting with an artist, provide tickets to the concert for the runners up so they don't go away empty-handed and you are recognized for being the "good guys". Also, do NOT let this type of stunt overpower your personality and become too much of your image. It's easy to create phone response and shocking reactions from listeners, but it's not an image with enduring value.

Why It **Works:** Who wouldn't be interested in watching someone eat a dozen worms through their nose? It attracts attention, even if it could be an audition for the circus!

1. Reduce the competitors before staging the event. If you have too many acts, the event takes a LONG time to complete, and you will end up with a lot of "minor" acts. Focus on 3-5 truly outrageous, interesting and mass-appeal acts that make great TV.

2. You are the ringmaster, not the sideshow! Don't become part of the act.

3. Find a convenient location with easy access for the public and the media. Newspapers love to cover this type of event.

4. It works best if the reason for the stunt is connected to civic pride or a celebration. In 1998, the Padres were challenging for the NL Championship. One of the most popular players was Wally Joyner, who was best recognized for his shaved head. Star 100.7 held a Wally Joyner haircut event, and shaved over 400 heads (including women).

   The "trigger" for this event was the fact that the Padres captured the hearts of San Diegans in this championship season. Star 100.7 managed to find the personality in the team to create a great event.

Who Should Do It:

If you don't mind contributing to a "silly" or "goofy" image, this type of event can be successful. It certainly gains attention. If a part of your character on the air is to be playfully immature, it is possible to use this effectively if managed properly.

One of the most effective uses of this idea can be in a simplified form. You identify the stunt to be performed, and have listeners compete for the prize as a "background" promotion during a show. For example, have 10 listeners drink a liter of water every 30 minutes. Last person who has to "pee" wins the prize!

Who Has Done It Before:

Almost every station that targets young males has performed some variation on this theme. Active Rock and Classic Rock stations are notorious for it, and many Alternative stations have made it a regular part of their arsenal.

-12-

BIZARRE LOVE TRIANGLE

This is a great "reality radio" bit that makes for compelling drama if it is executed properly. It's a simple idea but a very demanding stunt to pull off. It relies on finding three listeners who bring *personality* to you. If you get the wrong people, you're in trouble!

The idea revolves around finding a couple that has hooked up recently (within the last year or two). In exchange for a cash prize ($5,000 or more), they are asked to spend a week on display in public, in a king size bed. The twist is that they are joined for the week with one of the pair's "ex". All three of them! Can they last?

Personality: The character, traits, behavior of a person. Each person possesses unique qualities that he or she becomes known for.

How To Do It:

Find a shopping center, large furniture store, or other suitable, easy-to-access public location that will host the event. The participants will have to stay in bed for a full week, from 7am on a Monday morning through the end of your show Friday morning. If they make it, they get the cash!

When To Do It:

Anytime is fine, but make sure you're doing it when you

have no other major promotions on your station. For this to work, it has to capture the audience's imagination and take over all dayparts on the air. It must "ignite" and become the "talk of the town".

Pros:

It offers you a great opportunity to tell a story and generate publicity in the market. If the story catches on, you'll have great press and your listeners will help you spread the word. It's incredible grass-roots marketing.

Cons:

A *lot* of things can go wrong with this bit. It takes a lot of attention and air time to pull off properly. The participants must not only be willing to go along with it, but they also must have some genuine, deep feelings that will create conflict and controversy on the air. They must be dynamic personalities that allow their inner feelings come out on the air.

Watch Out For:

Genuine: Sincere, authentic, real, valid. It's a basic ingredient of a successful recipe.

One of the biggest challenges is finding a way to get into this bit. It must come up naturally on the air, and the "hook" must appear *genuine.* An option is to get into the topic of "sex with your ex", which leads to a "enter to participate" contest. You then choose the threesome that presents the best prospects for creating great radio.

Why It Works:

This bit creates great storyline "arcs". If you can hook the audience on your participating threesome, it'll be a home run. This stunt creates a situation where listeners are afraid to tune out, for fear that they will miss something.

It is a *must* that you make a "connection" with the participating personalities and your audience. They must have an interesting enough background to make a good story. Your recorded promos will be key in helping tell this story. The promos should describe the participants, their background, their personalities, and truly hook the audience on the drama of the story. Obviously, the story must be good, but your writing and creativity in telling the story is more critical.

Who Should Do It:

Stations that are skilled at telling stories and personalities that have enough confidence and focus to continue when it may feel like the bit is falling apart. This is one that requires intense commitment.

Who Has Done It Before:

B105 FM in Brisbane, Australia (Austereo) created this bit. PD Rex Morris' creative mind hatched the idea, and captured the imagination of the public.

Relationships make for great stunting. Another similar idea is to broadcast a divorce proceeding on the air...the whole nasty thing from breakup to completion. Every tear, every fight, every frustration. The station pays the legal costs.

-13-

HANDING OUT $100 BILLS

This is one of those promotions that you have probably heard of, and may have admired. If executed properly, it can be a wonderful way to get attention and create drama. It carries with it the risk of *backlash* when you reveal the source of the money, but the benefits usually outweigh the drawbacks.

Backlash: Repercussion, reaction, hostile response. For every action, there is usually an equal, and opposite, reaction!

How To Do It:

The morning personality dresses in a way that stands out, to capture attention. Some stations have used costumes, like a white tuxedo with dark glasses. Rent a limousine. Find areas where there are natural crowds gathered (community events or malls are perfect). The limo pulls up, your personality gets out and hands out $100 bills. Or, he walks into a restaurant and pays for unsuspecting customers' dinners. Do this a few times and people will start to talk. *Word of mouth* spreads and it eventually will find it's way into local media.

When To Do It:

The only time to do it is when you are new to the market, or are introducing a new personality to your show or station. This is a terrific promotion to gain pblicity and create *word-of-mouth* for a new personality.

Pros:

If this promotion is executed properly, and you are fortunate enough to gain some curiosity, it's better than a million-dollar marketing campaign. It offers the kind of attention and impact that marketing dollars can't buy.

Cons:

One of the problems with doing a promotion in the early days of your show's introduction is that the show may not be fine-tuned and ready to invite new listeners to the party! Be sure that when the audience tunes in you have a product that delivers. The first impression is always the most important. It also can be perceived as a negative from listeners if it comes off as a "cheap publicity campaign" to buy attention.

Watch Out For:

This promotion has been around for years, in various versions. Your competitors will likely be aware of it, and could take steps to thwart your effort. Still, what's the worst thing that could happen? Your show is out handing out cash to listeners-and that's still good publicity! Also be careful not to burn bridge with media outlets. If they feel manipulated or used, you risk future relationships. This is one of those times that you want to avoid contacting them about the story. They must be allowed to pick it up on their own.

Word Of Mouth: Publicity that spreads through your market

Why It Works:

A complete stranger handing out $100 bills? It's a home run! It makes for great bits on the air, even before the identity of the generous stranger is revealed. Executing it properly builds a story, a personality and an intrigue that you can cash in on much more effectively than just giving away cash.

Be sure you handle the event as if it were a typical, legitimate news story. This enhances the chances of obtaining publicity from your competitors. Don't let on tothe identity of the guy handing out the money. You can't even tell your staff what is going on. Only 2-3 people inside your radio station should know about it.

Who Should Do It:

There are various ways that the promotion could backfire, but if all goes well, it's a great way to become well known quickly. You have only one chance to get it done right…and it needs to be done with heavy activity in a short period of time.

Take major chances only when there's a lot to be gained! Superstar performers take a few risks, when the reward is worthwhile. If you spend too much time worrying about what could go wrong, you will miss opportunities!

-14-

FLAGPOLE SITTING

Whether the idea is literally sitting on a flagpole, or freezing yourself on ice, or submerging your show underwater, or any other marathon requires intense promotion and exceptional levels of personal commitment.

These promotions are normally staged to call attention to a charity or cause, and almost always are performed in order to break some sort of record. There are other ways to set "goals". The important factor is to establish a criteria for which you are striving.

How To Do It:

Regardless of how outrageous your idea, you have to start with a cause. Determine who will benefit, and what your angle is. Then, find the most public, visible location possible to hold your event. Shopping malls work well. Public parks can be good, and a local stadium or arena is often a good choice. Many stations choose to utilize a billboard in an area that receives high traffic. When choosing your location, consider three key aspects:

    1. How easy is it to broadcast from? You will be there for an extended period of time. Make sure that your

engineers can make the broadcast as comfortable as possible.

2. Does the public know instantly how to find you? If you have to explain how to find you, it will limit attendance. Also, remember that the more high profile locations usually add to the perception of "bigness" of the event.

3. Is it convenient for television crews to cover your story? Are you accessible? If your location is remote or difficult to reach, Assignment Editors will tend to pass over your story.

When To Do It:

There is no specific rule that governs the timing of these events. Some shows have created awareness by doing an "outside" promotion in the dead of winter to create a shocking reaction from listeners.

Pros:

It doesn't matter how many times it's been done, stunts that feature a personality doing something outrageous for a good cause always gets attention and generates publicity. It's also a good vehicle for demonstrating your "sensitive" side while explaining why you are putting yourself through the exercise!

Cons:

Even though you get good press, be careful about doing this too often. Most of all, be sure you focus on your *cause* rather than the *stunt*. The stunt is merely the mechanism you are using to benefit your cause. It's a great introduction to talking about the cause.

Stunt: Feat, exploit, deed, spectacular act.

Watch Out For:

I can't repeat this too often: Attempting a stunt like this requires that you have a cause for which to perform. If you don't have a *reason* for what you are doing, it will likely be regarded as merely strange, just another "wacky DJ bit". And God knows we have enough of those!

Reason: Motive, cause, basis, grounds, basis, rationale. A key ingredient in laying out a promotion.

Maintaining a proper balance during an extended stunt like this is difficult. To reach critical mass, it is required that you devote enough airtime to make the audience understand your mission. That's how you create a word-of-mouth "buzz" around the stunt. On the flip side, spending too much time on the "bit" takes you out of the routine that the audience expects from your show each day. This can be disruptive to listener patterns. You also run the risk of repeating your story to influence the cume, resulting in boredom from the core.

If you are including any kind of fund-raising in your promotion, be aware that listeners may have a "Jerry Lewis Telethon" mentality. Jerry raises hundreds of thousands of dollars for Muscular Dystrophy with his Labor Day telethon, which may perceptually make your effort sound small, even if you are successful in reaching your goal. It is key to remind listeners how you are making a difference and how their contribution matters. The public is desensitized. It's your job to raise their level of sensitivity.

Why It Works:

Especially if it's tied into a good cause, a stunt like this will be successful. Generally, listeners want to feel good about helping others, but it takes time and effort to do so. If you make it fun and easy for them to participate, they are entertained, and you've enabled them to feel good about themselves.

When attempting a stunt like this, whether it's raising money for charity or just doing something topical and outrageous to achieve a goal, there are several things that can make or break the event. First, it's important to constantly involve your listeners. Create a way for them to participate in the stunt. If you're raising money for a charity, that's easy. If not, however, you must find ways to make listeners feel a part of it.

Secondly, repeat the goal constantly, so you can demonstrate success along the way. If you're trying to raise $1,500 for a victim of a disaster, it may not sound like much. But if you show listeners that you have achieved your goal, you've been successful! Then, you can back-sell the celebration!

Third, constantly update listeners with a "running total" or progress. Listeners are tuning in and tuning out regularly. Make sure they can "find their place" when they tune in.

If your sales department is selling advertisers into your event, make sure you maintain control over all aspects.

Who Should Do It:

Most every show can execute some form of this stunt at some level. Remember, it doesn't have to be a major *campaign* like a telethon or marathon to be effective.

Who Has Done It Before:

Perhaps the most famous stunt of this type happened in the late 80's in Baltimore. The Orioles had lost their first 8 or 9 games of the season when the morning personality on a rock station decided to live on a billboard until the team won a game. Little did he expect that the O's would set a major league record by losing the first 21 games of the season, leaving him stranded for nearly two weeks! It created national attention, as well as a ton of local media.

More recently, one of KGB/San Diego's morning personalities, Abromowitz, applied the same idea to the pitiful 2000 Chargers. After losing their 10th straight game, he began living on the station's billboard, and stayed there for several weeks until the Chargers (finally) won a game. It attracted a lot of media attention, and was undoubtedly successful, but had less impact than the Orioles example because, with one game a week, there were fewer occasions of drama. The story only changed once a week instead of daily.

Campaign: Crusade, mission, war, drive. A true "campaign" is strategic, with promotions serving as tactical efforts to achieve the goal.

Plan stunts observing with your mission statement. For details on how to create an effective mission statement for your station and morning show, see *Morning Radio 1*, Chapter 3

Attention Programmers:

Whenever your talent takes a risk and it doesn't work out the way you had hoped or planned, take a deep breath, count to ten and relax before a meeting to discuss it. You're much better off if you commend more than criticize talent. Like a parent training a child, your most motivating tool is a pat on the back for good behavior. Too many times PDs are quick to criticize and slow to praise.

Part 2: Contests

Strategy & Execution of Games and Interactive Content to Extend Time Spent Listening

It is virtually impossible to spin the radio dial without finding a contest, and it is nearly as impossible to think of radio without thinking of contests. Our medium has traditionally been most successful using this marketing device. From a free lunch to a popular CD to a trip around the world to KIIS-FM and Rick Dees' $2 million contests, stations have attracted listeners, increased time spent listening and successfully "bought" listener loyalty, at least for the short term.

Recently, we've seen a trend moving away from morning personalities conducting regular contests, games and features. In the interest of being "real" and "spontaneous", many shows have turned into little more than stream of consciousness radio shows. Executed creatively, staged properly, and integrated effectively in the fabric of your show, *anyone* can make use of contests and games from time to time. If the game is devised within the framework of the show, it will work.

With so many contests on the air, and even the variety of options available to broadcasters, there must be good reasons for the explosion in on-air contesting. Let's take a closer look!

-15-

WHY HAVE CONTESTS?

E ven though research studies demonstrate that only 2-5% of your audience is likely to participate in a contest, consider the type of listener that a properly crafted contest attracts. Active listeners. Outgoing listeners. Listeners who participate. Now, think about the type of person that is likely to fill out an *Arbitron* diary.

However, the type of person who participates in contests is also less likely to have loyalty to one station. They have loyalty to contests! Whoever is giving away the best prize *right now* wins their participation. So your contest has to be the biggest, best and easiest to enter and win. *OR* it has to be the most entertaining for the non-participant to enjoy.

Consumers are more receptive to contests than ever before, which is both an opportunity and a challenge. It's an opportunity because you have a greater potential for achieving your goals than ever. It's a challenge because *everyone* is contesting. Contesting mechanics have improved. Payoffs are greater. Increased competition raises the stakes, and makes it more difficult to successfully draw that audience that your desire.

Before entering the Contest Zone, consider all of the elements and reasons to stage a contest.

> Arbitron: A research company, based in Maryland, that measures the audience of radio stations. Sometimes referred to in unflattering terms such as "Arbitrary"

Most of the time, contests on the air do not increase your product sampling. Don't confuse contesting with marketing. There are exceptions of course, but for the most part stations should not expect an increase in listeners because of any contest.

cume: a derivative of the word "cumulative". The total number of people who listen to a particular radio station in a specific time period, usually measured by the week.

A contest *can* generate cume if it is so well targeted that it connects with the audience and causes a market buzz. Large cash giveaways and fantasy prizes have the potential to accomplish this, though they must be *very* large to create attention in our society that is inundated with multi-million dollar lottery awards. Or, you can create new *cume* if the contest addresses community needs or social concerns.

So, if your contest may not increase the cume, it must be a TSL contest, right? One of the most popular reasons to stage contests is to improve time spent listening. Since it's been proven that TSL is largely a result of frequent occasions of listening, contests performed regularly, often and consistently are effective. While it is difficult to measure the actual affect contesting has on listener behavior, properly designed contests are a valuable tactic in playing the "quarter hour" game.

Perhaps the best use of contesting is to increase the profile of a station or personality against a competitor. The way a contest is designed, the appeal of a prize, the excitement of the winners and the fun of playing all contribute to the mood and feeling a listener receives from the station. It's a great way to brand your station.

Another possible benefit is to design a contest to enhance your image. Before a station or morning show can successfully create loyal fans, the audience must first understand the station or show. Contesting can help establish an image, develop an image, position your image, or enhance the image among listeners by communicating product advantages over others.

It's true that consumers choose products *emotionally* rathe than *logically*. Advertising expert Roy Williams explores this in his book "The Wizard of Ads" with the point that people choose things based on their emotions, and then justify their purchases based on intelligence. They choose neighborhoods and cars based on how they imagine themselves in those areas. They seek out Starbucks rather than drinking "ordinary" coffee because Starbucks has reinforced a great image of quality. Starbucks has convinced us that they are better than other coffees.

How does that affect your morning show? You should target everything on your show, including your contests, tc enhance your show and station image. Your morning show "*brand*", if you will. If you have a show that seeks to portray a self-image of an upscale adult listener, don't do a "most outrageous" contest or ask listeners to do things tha will embarrass them. Design all of your contests to contribute to your desired image.

Great contests like "The Phrase That Pays" have been usec as promotional tools to appeal to listener greed AND programming tools to establish a positioning statement in the minds of listeners. Crafting a contest to enhance your image is a difficult challenge, but one that pays off

Brand: In recent years, "branding a product has become the industry buzz. It is the Implanting of an associative memory in combination with a recall cue. Examples of successful "brands" are everywhere. You don't reach for a tissue, you reach for a "Kleenex". You never cover a cut or scratch with a plastic strip, you put on a "band aid". Brands exist only in the minds of listeners. To achieve "brand status", you must deliver your message and image consistently and frequently over a period of time. Branding takes patience. Are you truly *branding* your show, or merely promoting and marketing it?

handsomely if executed properly. Does your show depend on music? Be sure you are giving away tickets to every hot concert in town. Are you funny? Make sure your contests have an element of humor in it. Are you irreverent? Design the contest with an element of irreverence.

If you have already firmly established your image, contests can help build loyalty to your show and station by providing the active and passive entertainment listeners' desire. By giving away desirable prizes, you can identify with your listeners' lifestyle. Properly executed contests fulfill the fantasy of both the contest winner and non-winner if staged properly. In fact, many programmers are abandoning contests designed only to appeal to an audience's greed factor. The station that gives away the most money simply wins 'biggest prize" images. The station that tapes into its' audience's lifestyle creates desirable "prize" images *and* increases the entertainment on the air. This creates a psychological connection between you and the consumer, which is much more valuable than appealing to a specific demographic only. In fact, the secret to commanding dominant ratings is crossing demographic lines and appealing to a broad range of ages. This is achieved by appealing to a life group, not demographic target. Over time, focusing your contests on lifestyle groups will lead to tremendous goodwill. This goodwill leads to top of mind awareness, which pays off when the listener fills out a diary.

Finally, contests can generate revenue. Face it. Radio has changed and it's not a perfect world. You can fight this change, or you can embrace it. Change is neither good or bad. It just *is*.

Advertisers come to us to promote their business and your sales department (and GM) insists on airing value-added promotions to generate revenue. Accept it and figure out a way to accommodate the promotion requests. Many times, the advertiser demands are not consistent with your target, but it's up to YOU to figure out how to make it work! You may not think it's the best reason to air a contest, but it's reality, it's a problem, and you're probably going to be in a position of having to find a solution.

Speaking of targeting, many stations "overtarget" and only look at their appeal as demographic. Listeners (and consumers) choose products and morning shows based on emotional influences, not simply on objective data. Listener choices are not made in a laboratory, comparing their options. They are made when you reach out and touch the listener emotionally in their lives.

-16-

SERVICING YOUR CUSTOMER!

When listeners win prizes on your show, do they have to come to the station to pick up their prizes? In the interest of customer service, shouldn't it be more convenient for listeners to interact with you? If they can order practically anything in the world online and have it arrive at their door less than 48 hours later, you should be able to get prizes in their hands in a way that saves them time and eases their life.

Why not mail prizes to listeners, along with a note from the air personality thanking them for listening? If it's a larger prize, you should deliver it in person by an intern or promotions person in a station vehicle. Better still, go along for the ride and sign autographs and take pictures of the winner with you!

If you can't afford the time/money for that, trade-out or hire a courier service to deliver the prizes. You not only create additional goodwill, you attract attention to the station when a prize is delivered into offices and workplaces. Your station will stand out from the others. The listener is the most important person in our business. We depend on them. By treating listeners with the special-ness that they deserve, you will create the desire to listen again, listen more frequently and recommend your station to others.

The recurring theme in *Morning Radio* and in this book is that to be successful on the air or in any business that relies on customer service, evoking emotion and passion is necessary. If your listeners are truly *passionate* about your station, they are much more likely to remember you when they fill out the diary.

Passionate: Fervent, ardent, zealous, avid, fanatical. This is how you would like to describe your audience!

Alan Mason of the Audience Development Group calls this creating "Magic Moments" and relates an example of how Disney employees are trained to make each visitor's experience truly special.

A family wanted to celebrate their child's birthday at one of Disney's famous "character" breakfasts, but the family was late and missed their seating. The later shows were full. The family was sitting outside the breakfast, looking dejected, when a Disney employee noticed them.

The employee asked what was wrong and told them he would see what he could do. Knowing that kids with parents are the core target for Disney, and it was vital to the park's success to entertain the core target if they were to maintain their loyalty over other entertainment outlets, the employee was able to arrange a front-row table and have the boy's favorite character sing Happy Birthday to him.

You might expect that this employee was an executive, or at least a department head, at Disney. He was a custodian! He was doing his part, sweeping up, when he noticed what was going on and got involved. He knew that serving the audience was the responsibility of every employee at

Listeners will not be passionate about your station until you are passionate about your job. You can't have one without the other.

Disney, so he went out of his way, and out of his job description, to create a "Magic Moment".

Production value can be over-emphasized. Great song writers usually spend far more time on the production (melody) than on content (lyrics).

From The Desk Of...Scott Shannon.

"Great radio stations are not built on hot clocks and contests. They are built on heart"

-Scott Shannon is part of the Scott & Todd morning show on WPLJ/New York, and one of the most respected programmersin radio history.

-17-

SHOULD *YOU* HAVE CONTESTS?

S hould you contest? If so, how much? If you're debating how much contesting to use, consider that small contests usually generate more clutter than entertainment. The entertainment is in the presentation, *production value,* creativity and imagination that is relevant *to the audience.*

For a contest to be considered worthwhile, it must motivate and/or entertain a lot of people. Remember, people listen to the radio to be entertained, not to win tickets!

Whether or not to contest is at least partially an upper-management decision, but there are several issues to consider:

1. **Stations tend to over-contest.** Promotion Directors and Program Directors alike tend to over-contest because it's easy and they feel it's expected. DJ's become reliant on having a stash of prizes to give away. It makes the phone ring and gives them something to talk about, even if it's not particularly entertaining.

2. **Stations are intimidated by "running clean".**

Broadcasters often keep stale, worn-out contests on the air because they are uncomfortable without the hype on the air, or out of concern that their competition may use an idea against them. This insecurity leads to a cluttered station. As an industry, we love the flashy pomp and circumstance, the bells and whistles, the big show. The sexier the idea, the better we like it. But even great ideas may not be right for your station at a given point in time. Remember that listeners come to your station for the entertainment **first,** not your contests.

3. **Stations place too much emphasis on the contest.**
   When you're in the trenches every day, handing out money and backstage passes, it's hard to not get caught up in the excitement of the contest. Many programmers and personalities take the contest far too seriously. Be sure that the contests work for YOU, and you don't work for the contest. Contests may be a hook that gets consumers to sample your product, but the product itself is the primary motivation to listen. How many times do you hear a personality start a winning contest call with "Hi, you're caller number ____ "? the number caller is irrelevant to the *listener*, and the personality is wasting an opportunity to generate more excitement from the winner and entertain the audience.

4. **Contests are overused.** We've become so accustomed to contesting, we feel naked without it. Ask yourself "Why are we doing this?" Is it effective? Is there a strategic reason for this particular contest to be on the air? Do we need it? What would happen if it went away? What would replace it? Don't keep a contest on the air just because it's an easy solution. Easy solutions

are tune outs, and in our increasingly competitive business, tune outs are lost opportunities.

5. **Contests develop personality.** Your contests are helping develop station images. Contests can be fun, entertaining or in some cases, controversial. They help define the flavor of your station or your personality. Executed properly, they can be a tremendous assistance in developing long-lasting positive images. Or, they can lead to negative images like *too much talk,* too many commercials, or too much hype. Do your contests sound like commercials? Many do. Don't let contesting replace your personality as the primary source for developing stationality. **Stations lack creativity.** Don't slap a contest on the air just because you don't know what to do next! Have a plan! Don't make knee-jerk decisions. Contesting is tactical. Marketing is strategic. Know the difference and utilize contesting as part of the marketing effort.

6. **Ignore your competition.** It is common to keep tactics on the air in reaction to competitive pressures. Have the discipline to step back and evaluate the contest objectively through the experiences of a listener!

7. **Keep it in Perspective.** When constructing any contest or promotion on or off the air, remember that 100% of your audience samples you *on* the air, but far fewer participate at events. Yet more time and effort is often placed on off-air promotions and events than on the product itself.

To be effective, learn to distinguish between short-term challenges and true tactical opportunities. Avoid the mistake of offering a contest just to fill out your daily planner. Use contesting opportunities for the right reasons. It's just one of the solutions to a well planned marketing strategy. Use contesting for specific purposes and specific solutions to specific challenges.

What is "too much talk"? It's *any* talk that fails to relate to the audience. Even on music stations, talk is not bad-IF it entertains the audience. Talk that does not relate is just plain boring. And boring is *always* bad.

Morning personalities Mark & Mercedes (KMXB/Las Vegas) credit their success: "We make the listeners the stars. The listeners are our supporting cast. They keep it rolling."

From The Desk Of...Fran Lebowitz

"Radio news is bearable. This is due to the fact that while the news is being broadcast the disc jockey is not allowed to talk."

Fran Lebowitz, US Journalist in the 1950's

-18-

LEARNING FROM "MILLIONAIRE"

In 2000, the TV game show *Who Wants To Be A Millionaire* captured the world's imagination while competing game shows failed to achieve the same popularity. Now, game shows have been around for years and there is nothing particularly magical about the mechanics of this one over others. So why did "Millionaire" become the most watched TV show in prime time each night during the Spring Nielsen sweeps?

Well, start with the fact that the prize had a lot of appeal. Instant riches. Incredible wealth. One million dollars just for playing a trivia game. Secondly, the producers created an aura around the show that made it seem like *anyone* and *everyone* had an equal chance to be on the show. The method of qualification included inviting everyone to play a version of the game on any touch-tone phone.

The game itself is easy to play along with. They ask easy questions to raise the stakes, then the questions become increasingly difficult. All of the questions are multiple choice. The rules are simple and straightforward. It's easy to play, and more importantly, it's easy to *play along at home.*

That brings us to the host of the show. Regis Philbin understands the appeal of the game, and realizes his role in making the show a success. He never upstages the game, but rather adds to it. He explains the rules clearly, simply and logically (and repeatedly). He asks the questions with enthusiasm, drama, clarity and consistency. .

Furthermore, Regis cheers for the contestants. Watching the show, you get the feeling that Regis really wants the contestant to win $1 million. He never puts them down, never belittles them, no matter how poorly they perform. Regis has mastered the art of shining the spotlight on his subjects! In doing so, he receives all the credit for being a star!

Watching "Who Wants To Be A Millionaire", you wonder why Regis makes so much money doing it. His job is simple. Anyone could do it. But therein lies the secret. It's his simplicity, his character, his consistency, his delivery and his professionalism in not upstaging his contestants. Regis is sincere. He's not trying to upstage the contestants.

Regis is so *likable*. Everybody loves him, from college girls to 70 year-old women. It's not because of his big voice. And his accent is annoying! He's friendly, doesn't try to be some-thing he is not and doesn't take himself too seriously. He's down-to-earth and never comes off as being overly cool, or above the audience!

The result is that everybody – absolutely *everybody* – loves Regis!

Now, compare the way Regis conducts his game show with the way a typical morning show presents theirs. It's a stark contrast. Most morning shows are obsessed with being the stars. They try to put all the emphasis on themselves. They constantly upstage the contestant and the content. When you conduct a contest on the air, remember the example set by Regis and the producers of the most popular game show since "Let's Make a Deal" (another show that was wildly successful because the host, Monty Hall, knew how to construct the contest).

Be original. Reject the notion of "one size fits all". Learn from the principles of great programmers and personalities, but remember that greatness never came from conformity.

Big changes can only occur when you accept some risk. If you try and eliminate risk, you will find that the opportunity no longer exists.

-19-

GAINING CREDIBILITY

Regis has been such a wildly successful personality in part because of the "down home" nature in his presentation. You see, in many ways, you tell your listeners what you think of them…every morning, every hour, every break. They can sense it when you think of them as a large mass of audience, used to provide an object for your own perceived brilliance.

They also sense it when you act in a caring way, concentrating on THEIR needs and wants. If you want your listener to LIKE you instead of merely tolerating you, learn from the personality demonstrated by Regis.

1. Respect their intelligence. Avoid using big words, flaunting your intelligence, when smaller words will work. Don't show off, don't patronize, and assume that your listener is just as smart as you are-but they may not be paying as much attention.

2. Deliver on your promises. Be direct, to the point. Don't promote a giveaway "coming up", then, not run it for an hour. Be responsible. Don't assume that nobody will notice. If you absolutely can't deliver on a promise, apologize for it and explain

See *Morning Radio*, Chapter 4

how you will make it up.

3.   Be unpredictable. Some of the best moments of
     "Millionaire" happen when Regis steps out of
     "format for just a moment. Step out of your radio
     persona. Be a real person.

4.   Show enthusiasm when talking to listeners both on
     and off the air. Talk to anyone who has seen Regis
     Live, and they will tell you that they are most im-
     pressed by how hard he works to endear himself to
     the audience *during the commercials.* He's always
     "on", and his audience loves him for it! Listeners
     form an impression of you based on how you treat
     callers on the air, and they are observing you in
     public.

5.   Stay fresh. It's like a marriage that starts out with a
     lot of sparks only to have the newness wear off and
     become monotonous. One of the challenges on
     "Millionaire" was keeping the public interested after
     the novelty wore off. Their decision to have celebri-
     ties playing for their favorite charities was one
     remedy. You have to work on new material, new
     devices and new angles to entertain your audience.
     Otherwise, they become bored.

6.   NO inside jokes or jargon. You have to enter your
     listener's world, not expect to bring them into yours.
     Listeners don't know, or care, what is happening
     internally, behind the scenes. They just want to be
     entertained. Also, every time you refer to something

that has gone on before, such as a running gag, you must explain it to your listener as though it were the first time they heard it. It doesn't have to be long and involved, just enough to set the stage.

To relate and be one-to-one with your audience, you have to take care of them and put THEM first...not yourself.

Think about it. On your best day, only 3% of your audience will physically participate in your contest. In the course of a full week, maybe 7-10% will bother playing your contest. Design your contests with the nonactive participant in mind.

Dress up your contests with some sizzle! "Who Wants To Be A Millionaire" is a much more exciting name than "Regis Philbin's Trivia Challenge". Apply the same brainstorming process to your contests.

-20-

REMEMBER WHO YOU SERVE

One of the reasons that Regis is successful is his focus on who he *serves*. He is a master of making the viewer, the audience-comfortable.

In the days when an ice cream sundae cost much less, a ten-year old boy entered a hotel coffee shop and sat at a table. A waitress put a glass of water in front of him.

"How much is an ice cream sundae?", he asked.
"Fifty cents," replied the waitress.

The little boy pulled his hand out of his pocket and studied the coins in it. "Well, how much is a plain dish of ice cream?", he inquired. By now more people were waiting for a table and the waitress was growing impatient. "Thirty-five cents," she brusquely replied."

The little boy again counted his coins. "I'll have the plain ice cream," he said. The waitress brought the ice cream, put the bill on the table and walked away.

The boy finished the ice cream, paid the cashier and left. When the waitress came back, she began to cry as she wiped down the table. There, placed neatly beside the empty dish, were two nickels and five pennies — You see, he couldn't have the sundae, because he had to have enough left to leave her a tip.

When performing *your* show, remember to tip your listeners. Tip them generously and frequently, and they'll give you *great* service.

The best way to enhance your time spent listening is to increase the "occasions" of listening. In other words, creating moments that cause listeners to tune in frequently is often better than enticing them to listen for longer periods of time. Pre-promotion is your best tool to creating those occasions of listening. Effective promotion of your contests should lead to stronger top-of-mind awareness, which multiplies the odds of listeners "making an appointment" with your station at a particular time. That's serving your listener!

Have a standard series of lines you would like listeners to say about your show and station. After a contest, ask the winner to record a line for you. They'll be naturally more enthusiastic and you'll get a great "read" for your drop.

-21-

Principles of Great Contests

1. The contest must be simple and easy to play. It has to be easy to play along with in the car, or at work, and interesting to the casual listener.

2. Design the contest with the listener in mind, not the participant. This is entertainment. Don't get caught up in the game itself. Focus on the entertainment.

3. Carefully screen contestants to add to the entertainment value. Contestants don't HAVE to be random callers, or the 10th caller gets to play, etc. Most stations resort to the XXth caller out of convenience. You should solicit for contestants who are interested in playing the game, and choose the best callers. Look for enthusiastic, fun and likable callers who sound great. The type of contestant that your listeners will CHEER for, and celebrate when they win. Nothing kills a game more than an unexcited winner. Some of the most successful TV game shows of all time thrived by looking for contestants that were slightly below the typical intelligence level of the average listener. How many times have you shouted out the answer to the puzzle in "Wheel of Fortune" when the contestants just haven't

Understand Your Audience's Lifestyle. *Morning Radio I* **Chapter 5**

quite figured it out yet? It makes the home player feel good about them, and participate with the show with more regularity. Conversely, think how frustrating it would be if the questions were always answered before you "got" it.

4. Prepare the contestants. Your producer or screener should insure that the contestants understand how to play the game, what the rules are.

5. The host of the game is not the star. The contestants and the game must be in the spotlight. The host stays out of the way, careful not to upstage the contestants. The host must stay focused and not become distracted away from the game. Ego kills contests, and destroys morning shows.

6. It's the GAME, not the PRIZE. The prize can be important to the ultimate success of the game, but it's the execution of the game itself that provides the "play at home" value. If you make the game fun to play, listeners will

Just because you sound good does not mean you will perform well in Arbitron. Creating entertainment that leads to listeners casting your votes for you is the key to success.

From The Desk Of...Jim Abrams

"A smart morning show will learn from their mistakes, and never make it again. A wise morning show finds a smart morning show and learns how to avoid the mistakes they made."

(paraphrased from a quote about business)

---

participate, regardless of the prize. In some cases, you'll get BETTER contestants with little, or even no, prizes.

7. Quick intros and setups get you into the game, and the entertainment value, more quickly. The contest must be quick and easy to explain, so you can quickly get to the game, which provides the entertainment. Remember the Kiss theory...KEEP IT SIMPLE STUPID!

8. Dramatic payoffs. Build to the moment of truth. Have a dramatic conclusion. Great contests like "Battle of the Sexes" create drama and/or conflict. KCBQ/San Diego's Jack McCoy demonstrated this with the legendary "Last Contest" some years ago. Though the prizes offered were outstanding, the appeal was in the production and the drama the contest inspired.

Be patient! Just as a farmer plants in the spring, nurtures the crop throughout the growing season, and reaps the harvest in the fall, you must invest your time and efforts in areas that will pay off. You may be able to accelerate the growing season, but the best results are achieved when you allow the crops to become fully mature!

Hook, setup, dress up, payoff and blackout are the five steps in building a bit. For details, refer to *Morning Radio I*, Chapter 8

-22-

PRIZES

Not every station has an unlimited budget to hand out thousands of dollars in prizes for your morning show contests. In fact, it's more likely that you're stuck with giving away a year's supply of Mrs. Cubbison's dressing!

Sure, the greater the incentive in your contests, the greater the expected response. But having the biggest budget, or an unlimited amount of cash has nothing to do with the actual success or effectiveness of your contests. Get over it!

When putting together your contests, use your imagination. It's much better to give away items that your listeners can't get at any price than it is to hand out big dollar prizes.

Be creative. Don't just hand out tickets to see the latest Ricky Martin concert. Make some phone calls, use some favors and find a way to give away Ricky's PANTS.

Average: Normal, usual, typical, run-of-the-mill, ordinary, routine. BORING.

Never give away anything *average*. Give away something VERY LARGE ($10,000 cash or a dream vacation) or VERY SMALL (a gallon of Mustard), but never average. Extremes get more attention. You can entertain listeners with the smallest, most mundane prizes. It can be great fodder for the show.

The three best prizes that appeal to the most people?

1. Cash
2. Cash
3. Cash

Nothing else is close. As many listeners will go out of their way to win $1,000 as they will to win a trip around the world or a new car. It's great to offer a big prize, but you'll reach the same level of added cume by sticking with the cash! Money talks!

However, not everyone is blessed with a huge cash budget for contesting. Don't be disheartened. Remember, it is better to have an effective contest than to have a popular contest. Give away prizes listeners can't buy. Anyone can give away tickets to a concert. YOU should give away DINNER with the performer!

Make your prizes *special*. Think like a listener. What is special to them? It could be something as easy to obtain as an autographed album or guitar. How about having dinner with your morning show? Or how about tickets for a family to go to a local theme park? Or even a zoo? Listeners appreciate these prizes more than you know. Radio people take too many things for granted, and miss opportunities to create valuable prizes for listeners.

Popular contests and effective contests are NOT the same. Contests are usually popular because they offer big bucks. Effective contests entertain and engage your audience.

-23-

REGULAR CONTESTS

Daily features can be one of the most difficult types of on-air content for a show to implement. Those daily, repetitive features soon become stale, boring and mundane to the talent. The personalities lose interest, don't take them seriously and fail to maximize their impact.

It's true that a lot of features are basically "throw away" items. They are monotonous, easy to execute and can become boring. But to a listener, these same features are benchmarks in their day, eagerly anticipated entertainment elements that they understand and look forward to. How long has David Letterman been performing his Top 10 List each night at the same time in the show? It's one of the all-time classic features that has defined his personality and place in American pop culture.

Many personalities never become known for anything because they don't stick with their features long enough. They get bored, distracted and impatient waiting for the audience to respond and "catch on" to what they are doing. Then, just as listeners are starting to become interested, they discard the feature for something else, and the process begins anew.

-24-

TEACHING YOUR AUDIENCE

I t's easy for us to forget that, though we are in the entertainment business, we're really in the business of *teaching audiences* what we are and what we do. We get too caught up in "inside thinking" and assume that listeners understand what we're all about. Many times, they don't retain our call letters and frequency, let alone our personalities names, programming features and promotions.

Radio is usually a secondary focus for listeners, particularly in the morning. They are dealing with traffic jams, working, getting the family off to work and school, preparing breakfast, reading the morning newspaper and any number of other things that distract them from listening attentively.

These distractions inhibit your audience from getting your messages. They fail to perceive because your show is just along for the ride. In addition, listeners tend to forget very quickly. They are bombarded with so many messages, most are simply discarded and forgotten.

So, when you build your features, there are several principles that will help you cut through the *"brain clutter"* and make an impact:

> **1. Make it clear and meaningful.** Be direct, clear

Clutter: Confusion, muddle. Too many messages, or messages presented in a disorganized manner will hamper your efforts to "cut through" with your message.

and get right to the point. Avoid the common mistake of assuming your audience knows what the feature is. Explain to them what you are doing.

2. **Focus on one or two main topics inside the feature**. Too many messages compete with each other for attention, and nothing will be retained. If you are doing an "entertainment news" feature, spotlight the one or two *best* stories that are most likely to have an impact. Move quickly through all the others in "headline" fashion.

Benchmark: A regularly scheduled element, performed consistently at regular intervals that become instrumental in helping listeners develop listening "habits".

3. **Repeat your features** over and over at the same times, at regular intervals. Repetition creates familiarity. Familiarity leads to retention. When the feature is retained, it becomes a *benchmark*. Benchmarks aid in recalling listening! And *that* is what creates higher ratings. Relate the message to your audience's lifestyle, needs, and usage. If your personal lifestyle and interests are out of sync with the target audience's, you have a problem. If you don't believe that repetition is an important factor in fitting into your audience's lifestyle, try this: On your next vacation, stay in town and live life as a "real" listener. You'll find out quickly how difficult it can be for listeners to follow the flow of entertainment on a radio show.

4. **Teach by example**. Use listener drops, phone calls and other production elements to teach

The value of repetition is emphasized in *Morning Radio 1*, chapter 5

your listeners how you want them to use your station. Many stations use winner promos to showcase their contests and teach listeners how the contests are played. Apply the same idea to your morning show.

This is not to suggest that you can take a weak feature and make it popular just by doing it consistently over a long period of time in a simple, direct, straightforward, clear and concise manner. Discipline is required to objectively evaluate each feature to determine its' value. Regularly review your on-air elements and ascertain whether they hold up as is, need to be reworked or should be dropped.

Performed properly, daily features like "Battle Of the Sexes" or weekly features like "Movie Reviews" can provide a backbone for your show. The challenge is to present them with an interesting, fresh enthusiasm each time.

When Abbott & Costello were hired by NBC Radio to do their show, they were bound in their contract to do their "Who's On First" routine at *least* once a month. That's the bit they were known for, the one that made people laugh. And that's what *worked*. Whether or not your show plays music, you still need to *play the hits*.

Rick Dees has built his career on straight forward, well-executed, relevant benchmark features like "Dees Sleaze" and Larry LuJack developed a benchmark that defined his show (Animal Stories) through proper pre-promotion.

-25-

THE LOST ART OF PRE-PROMOTION

P re-selling upcoming bits is an area most every show can improve on. Why do we promote our upcoming features on the air? Simple. To hook listeners on the value of what is coming up, motivate them to stay tuned, thereby maximizing *TSL* and increasing their perceived importance of your station in their lives. Become a part of their daily routine and they reward you with entries in their Arbitron diary. Great. How can you get that wrong? A lot of jocks do.

TSL: Time Spent Listening. The amount of time a listener spends listening to your radio station. Expressed in quarter hours. Combined with your cume, one of the key components in determining your ratings, and ultimately, your fate.

For a lesson in pre-promotion, study (don't just watch-*study*) network television programming. It's a constant barrage of creative, fresh pre-promotion for their upcoming programs. Their goal is to hook you on that next sit-com and coax another half hour of viewing. And they don't do it just once. They run multiple impressions, presented creatively, with enthusiasm each time. How can you apply their methods to promoting your show and your elements?

1. **Use audio**. Instead of just promoting "Battle of the Sexes", play a challenge from today's contestants. Instead of just saying that "Hollywood Gossip" is coming up, play a portion

of the clip of a celebrity in the news to hook the audience on the full story. Production value in your show will hold the listener's attention and stand out from the pack

.2. **Be creative**. Spend time crafting the pre-sell. Brainstorm it. Write it out. Pre-record it if you need to. Use audio, sound effects and approach the tease from multiple angles.

3. **Personalize it.** Make it meaningful to your listeners by creating a personal bond with them

4. **Sensationalize it.** How many times have you waited through an entire television newscast for that "kicker" story that was pre-promoted four times in 30 minutes, only to turn off the TV and say "I waited around for a half hour for *that.*" Ah, but the point is you *did* watch until the end of the news, and because of the pre-promotion, you're likely to *remember* what you watched. And, *recall* is 90% of success in the radio ratings game.

5. **Repeat the tease**. Sometimes it seems like "Entertainment Tonight" is more pre-promotion than content. Their pre-sells are so well crafted, that they become part of the entertainment value of the show.

Most air personalities are terrible at selling the listener on listening longer. You may express a distaste for anything related to sales, but when it comes right down to it, everyone on the air is a salesperson. Now, ask any salesperson the key to successful selling and the conversation will eventually lead to the concept of creating the desire for your product in the minds of the prospect. You are selling your product to a consumer. Creating the desire for the product is the art of pre-promoting your content. If you fail to effectively sell the benefits of your station, your show and your personality, the result is lost sales.

Moreover, nearly every personality in America is just going through the motions with little enthusiasm or excitement when it comes to promoting the station.

When you construct any promotion, feature or bit, you must isolate the most important and compelling aspects of your material and ask yourself, "What can I say about this that will cause my listener to want to hear more, react or participate?"

Ask yourself, "How can I turn the events of the next half hour into dramatic, anticipated entertainment?"

Here are some examples:

WEAK: Hi, this is (your name here). We're here til 10 this morning...and next half hour, we have Hollywood Sleaze, right before the news.

EFFECTIVE: I'm (your name here). (Midday DJ) is on at 10 today with Phil Collins, Matchbox 20 and more of your requests during the No Repeat Workday. (Madonna hook starts in background) Now, coming up in less than 20 minutes, (news person) will tell you who Madonna is considering to take with her on her upcoming tour....you won't believe it! That and more on Hollywood Sleaze at 7:45"

WEAK: We're taking a break and we'll be back after this (don't laugh, I hear this going into stop sets *all the time)..*

EFFECTIVE: Now, if you're stuck in traffic, we'll tell you why....and if you're just leaving the house, we'll warn you about the trouble spots in just a minute...and, in about 10 minutes, we'll tell you which movies parents took their kids to most this weekend-I think you'll be surprised!

WEAK: Coming up, we'll have a check on weather, sports and today's Battle Of the Sexes.

EFFECTIVE: The new weather forecast is out, and it looks great for the weekend...I'll have that next....and at 8:10, Mandy is back representing the women in Battle Of the Sexes....she beat David yesterday with this question (play audio). Battle of the Sexes is coming up.

WEAK: Another Candid Phone call, the word of the day and much more coming up.

EFFECTIVE: At 7:25, we have another candid phone call...this one is to an exterminator in (town) that (premise of call)...you won't believe it...and it's coming up in less than 30 minutes.

Promotion means selling. Provide relatable material that really means something *to the listener*. Give them a chance to WANT to listen to what you have planned.

As talent coach Karen Young points out in an article in *Morning Mouth,* it's all about creating feelings in your listeners. Syndicated host Delilah is a master at using words to evoke strong emotions. Don't waste your opportunities to connect with your listener when you tease upcoming elements.

Advertisers normally assume that their message needs to be heard at least three times in a relatively short period of time (a week) to be effective. The most dynamic ad campaigns are designed with an appreciation for how to use repetition. Your morning show must grasp the same principles.

-26-

MAKE IT SHOW BIZ

Radio has so many lessons to learn from the methods used to build anticipation for a new show, series or episode. The drama and excitement leading into a season ending "cliffhanger" is almost always more interesting than regular episodes of the show. Your show should use some of the same principles to build an expectation for your features and bits.

Presenting your elements as if you're reading a checklist doesn't cut it! You have to put some time and effort into the *marketing* of your bit, element or feature. Consider your show a marketing challenge, not a programming challenge. The programming is your content and entertainment elements. If you want those elements to really cut through and *sizzle,* you have to dress them up the way television markets their programs.

You are working in an auditory medium. You are also working in the entertainment industry. Your power of persuasion (convincing people to listen to you, to be entertained by you) is not an exercise in accuracy, but in creating drama. Accuracy and literal interpretation is for the journalists covering stories for the newspapers and evening news. The possibilities for your show are without limit if you use your imagination.

Marketing: Multistep process that begins with product creation/development, continues through promotion and advertising. The successful end of your marketing results in causing a response

That means creating content that is exciting and dramatic, punctuated with highlights and production elements that enhance the listener's anticipation. Dress it up. This is show biz!

Evaluate any character voices you do on your show. If you're still doing Johnny Carson or Ronald Reagan voices on your show, just because you're good at it, you're missing the connection with the audience. Every element on your show should go through the "relevancy" test regularly.

-27-

EXPAND YOUR HORIZONS

It's easy to do the same old, same old. Everyone has the database of "today in history" and birthday lists, and some shows have been doing these in the same old tired way since 1983. You can easily get all the latest Hollywood Gossip any time. How is *your* execution of Hollywood Gossip going to stand out and be different from the next guys? If some show in your market hasn't done, or isn't currently doing "Battle of the Sexes" you probably are working in a third world country. These all can be effective bits, but what have you created lately that provides your listeners a fresh benchmark for remembering you?

To avoid falling into a rut, all entertainers must force themselves to do something different. Do something new. The public grows tired of the routine very quickly, unless it is one of your benchmarks. This week's hot movie and actor is yesterday's news next month. Listeners crave change, seek change, demand change, and they count on you to keep them in touch.

Consider how life has changed in the past few years. It's faster paced, more demanding. The microwave just won't cook your food fast enough anymore! Communication, home accessories, homes, the work place and television have all undergone dramatic changes because the public has created new requirements in the way life is lived. Listeners are constantly seeking new, fresh stimulation. If your features and on-air material fail to adapt to the changes in society, you're doomed to becoming obsolete. Be bold. Be creative. Do things differently! Take some risks, and be alert enough and smart enough to know if something is working or not.

How do you get out of your normal patterns and see things differently? Change your routine. Instead of picking up *People* magazine this week, get an issue of *Spin*. Read a local newspaper from another part of your city or state. Do anything you can to get another perspective on life and on society. It may not directly change the way you deliver material on your show, but it will affect the way you think. It may be just the fresh approach you need.

Research has proven that even a fatigued <u>good</u> contest produces better results than a fresh, "other" contest. Frequently, it's the station personnel who think a contest is tired when listeners are still very interested. The great TV game shows like Wheel Of Fortune and Jeopardy are perfect examples. The ability to remain consistent and fresh is a delicate balance.

At the peak of your success, look for things you can do even better. In other words, attack yourself regularly. Keep pushing yourself!

-28-

GOOD-DAY!

How do you stay relatable in the listener's world? Take a lesson from the master, Paul Harvey. Now in his 80s, his content is just as relevant in this century as it was for the last half of the last one. Harvey says, "My biggest challenge is to keep intellectually articulate and pliable enough to adapt to inevitable change. I may not enjoy rap music, but I need to *know* about it, and it's function if I am going to deal with contemporary news".

Today, listeners require you to not only stay in touch with their world, but to deliver your material in a more concise package than ever before. Their attention span is a maximum of 30 seconds, so if you don't get to them quickly, you'll lose them. Interview segments, sound bites, and an increasing emphasis on the preciousness of our *time* raises the challenge of appealing to the audience quickly and driving home your point instantly. Here again, Harvey sets a great example to follow. His delivery is consistent, familiar and comforting. His trademark "Page 2" and "Good Day" comments add formatic structure to the show.

If your features and contests are familiar to your audience, it can facilitate getting to the entertainment more rapidly, and increase your chances of appealing to your listener.

-29-

CONTEST LIBRARY

Here is a list of popular contests you can use or adapt for your show! Some of these may seem too "big" or not within your budget, but be creative and adapt them to your situation!

Dollar Bill Game
Playing games with dollar bills works every time. It's easy to play, everyone gets involved, and is interactive. One version of the "Dollar Bill Game" is simply spending a dollar bill in a grocery store or convenience store, then read the serial number the next morning and award the first caller who has the bill free cash ($100 or more). Take this to the next level by taking out insurance for a major payoff of $100,000 or even $1 million. SCA Promotions will help you insure this contest - visit them at scapromotions.com You can also have listeners play various versions of the game at designated times who have a dollar bill with any form of your frequency in the serial number (this one is great for appearances or events too) or any number of creative combinations.. Make sure they bring in the dollar bill for verification.

Beat The Bomb
You might want to rename this game in light of world problems, but for our purposes here, we'll deal with the

classic contest as made famous on KIIS-FM and other great stations. A caller tries to collect as much cash as possible before the bomb explodes. Start the game with a sound effect of a clock ticking, and a voice which announces increasing dollar amounts every few seconds. Start low and increase the amount by varying amounts. Make sure the bomb explodes at different intervals each round. If the bomb explodes before the listener says, "STOP", they lose the money and win a smaller prize. If they say, "STOP" before the bomb explodes, they win the last cash amount announced. To make it big, make it the $10,000 Beat the Bomb, with each contest having the potential of reaching up to $10k. this will actually save you money. Listeners will have a tendency to stay in longer, and will lose all the cash more often!

Cash, Cars and Stars
This is a winner on many levels, and is fun to play on the air. Solicit a caller, and award cash to the winning participant ($100). The person who wins the cash is then read a list of five hot cars and they choose the one they would like most. You also ask the person what celebrity they would like to deliver the car if they win the Grand Prize (enter their choices in the final drawing). You guarantee that their star will deliver it, or, if the star chosen is not available to the Grand Prize winner, offer extra cash instead ($5,000). Another variation is to offer the car to the person who identifies the 'stars' that are in the car, and where they are sitting, based on clues you give. This "theater of the mind" approach sustains for several weeks.

Double or Nothing

Here is a fun takeoff on "Who Wants To Be A Millionaire". Listeners test their trivia skills for a chance to win cash. Ask a series of questions and each correct answer will double the total prize money. Listeners can stop after any question and take the money or continue for double or nothing. If they get all of the questions correct they win a big cash prize (like $10,000). However, an incorrect answer leaves them with nothing.

Hands On

We've done this one at Star 100.7 several times. It always creates a lot of interest. Qualify 25 to 50 finalists (depending on the prize-a new car works best). Each finalist will have an opportunity to win if they can keep their hands on it the longest. Hold this event in a high traffic area. All contestants place their hands on the Grand Prize and keep them there the longest to win it. You can set the rules up however you like (one hand on or two hands on, length and frequency of breaks, etc.).

Big Money High/Low

Here's an oldie, but goodie! Start with a random amount of money, down to the penny. At designated times, listeners have an opportunity to call-in and guess the amount in your Jackpot. If the guess is correct, they win the money. If they're wrong, you tell them if they are too high or too low to help narrow down the jackpot amount. A new Jackpot starts once the previous jackpot is awarded.

Let's Make A Deal

It was one of the best game shows of all time! Hold your own version of on the air. The correct caller has to decide whether to take a guaranteed cash prize or pass on the cash and take a shot at one of two envelopes. The envelope may contain real prizes like trips, shopping spree, etc. OR, they may contain a smaller prize like a station key chain, bumper sticker, discount coupons, etc. This is also a great contest for appearances, remotes and events.

Say It and Win/Phrase That Pays

Give away cash and teach your listeners what you want them to remember about you. You create the slogan, they repeat it, and they win. Some uses: Every time a person can say your Phrase That Pays in (x) seconds wins. Example: "Z100 is New York's #1 Hit Music Station" . You can also hit the streets or make random phone calls and ask people at "What Station Do You Listen To Most?" If they say (your station phrase), award the cash.

From The Desk Of...Branch Rickey

"Give me the errors of enthusiasm over the base-hits of complacency, anytime"

Rickey is a legendary former exeutive with the Brooklyn Dodgers. He is responsible for bringing Jackie Robinson into Major League Baseball.

PART 3: FEATURES

IDEAS TO CREATE BENCHMARKS

-30-

WHY SHOULD YOU HAVE FEATURES?

Features are terrific elements that can help give your show structure, form and a consistency that helps your audience reconstruct their listening. That's a key benefit when it comes time to fill out that ratings diary!

Features can also be effective in showcasing specific members of the show that may play a minor role. Using a new, or seldom-used personality to be the main presenting personality on "Hollywood Gossip" will help develop the character and role of that personality in the minds of your audience. It helps to build and define the personality.

Some shows that are working together for the first time have a difficulty in developing chemistry on their own. Features can be a great way to help define roles and expectations between the personalities while the natural interpersonal relationship develops.

For programmers, features help with the show prep process for your talent. Too often, the programmer and air talent have different goals, or different interpretations of the goals for the show. Agreeing on several benchmark features provides a common ground and sense of comfort that can be the foundation for building trust as the show develops and grows. Well-designed features can help a new show gain some footing while learning their audience and giving their audience a chance to "get to know" them.

They give you a forum for relating to your audience and maintaining topicality consistently each morning. Face it, most of the time you have topics that you *know* you should talk about, but have no idea how to get it on the air. Letterman's Top 10 feature is not only entertaining, it helps keep Dave topical and relatable with what is happening in the world *that day*. Features can help you do the same thing on your show each day.

Finally, features provide content and unforgettable benchmarks! Benchmarks are valuable for helping listeners "reconstruct their listening behavior. And, in the ratings game, if your audience is able to reconstruct their listening by the features on your radio station, you stand a fighting chance of getting their "vote" in the diary, and helps tilt the balance your way in the fight for the elusive *phantom cume.*

The diary system of compiling ratings data will always reward those shows that create a "buzz". Research has shown respondents who have mentioned a contest or personality name, but when further questioned, reveal that they have not actually listened to that station personally. Other instances reveal that listeners will say "oh yes, I *always* listen to that station" but on further examination, we find that they actually listen only one or two days a week.

Phantom cume: Listening that goes unrecorded in the ratings services. There are two types of phantom cume: 1) Listening that takes place but is not measured in the ratings services because the audience fails to recall that listening, and 2) Credit for listening that does not actually take place. Great features that become benchmarks help you take advantage of this more desirable type of phantom cume!

-31-

WHEN SHOULD YOU AIR A FEATURE?

Features can air at any time in your show. Obviously, the better features should be programmed in hours that impact the greatest audience. One key, though, is that features should air at the *same time* each day, each week. I've heard the argument that strong features should "float", thereby exposing the best material to listeners who tune in at different times, but my experience is that the result of this tactic is that the feature fails to catch on and impact the audience.

A powerful feature brings with it the benefit of helping your audience remember you. The *best* features can become a part of your listener's routine. When a listener knows that "I have to be on the freeway, past the third exit by the time they start *Battle of the Sexes*", you know that your feature has become a "benchmark". Establish true benchmarks and you can count on your audience rewarding you with diary entries.

Make time your ally by working hard and maintaining your persistence.

So, then, it follows that the key to a successful feature is that it become a benchmark. This means that you must perform it regularly and consistently. Persistence and consistency will pay off over time.

A good idea is essential. Hard work is a given. But your persistence will usually bring success.

-32-

WHO SHOULD DO FEATURES?

Nearly every show can use some features, if they're designed properly and customized to the character and personality of the show. A better question is, "how *many* features should you do, and how do you balance the features with the other morning show elements and content?"

For new, developing shows, features can provide the structure and organization that gives substance while you develop personality and character. Established shows can use features as benchmarks that give listeners comfort and a point of reference to remember the show. Mature shows run the risk of hanging onto the same features for too long, as apathy begins to erode the impact of their features.

How many are right for you? There is no *correct* formula. In most cases, it is better to have slightly too *many* features than too *few*.

But beware! Features are like creeping vines that grow up the side of your house. One morning you wake up and they're growing all over your roof, and you wonder how it got out of control! It's important to regularly "prune" your show and use those features to enhance the beauty and appearance of your personality rather than overpowering it!

Your show is a dynamic, evolving work that should constantly be under development.

The feature ideas in this book are all proven winners, but may not be right for your show. As with all of your elements and content, select the right elements that maintains a consistent "feel" to your show. Presentation, production and delivery of the right elements leads to ultimate successful execution.

Self contained features normally work best, because of the way most listeners use the radio. Today's listeners are challenged for their time and attention.

From The Desk Of...Anne Frank

"The radio ... goes on early in the morning and is listened to at all hours of the day, until nine, ten and often eleven o'clock in the evening. This is certainly a sign that the grown-ups have infinite patience"

From "Anne Frank: Diary of a Young Girl"

-33-

HOW MANY, HOW OFTEN?

I s there such a thing as *too many* features? Some shows become so reliant on their features you hear little else. They swing from "Crooks are Stupid" to "Battle of the Sexes" to "Hollywood Gossip" to "Music Trivia" and never have time to relax and relate to the audience.

I worked with a morning show in a medium market that spent almost all of their time pre-promoting and executing their features. They did a good job with each individual element, but the show was lacking a natural-ness. The solution? We kept doing the features, games and contests but removed the *names* of some of the features. The result was that the show took on a much more spontaneous sound. It flowed naturally and comfortably while still providing the structure and discipline this developing show needed. For example, instead of launching into "Here's today's Topic Of the Day—call now", we introduced the segment by simply creating a story that transitioned into a topic that led to phone calls. Same result, same structure. But a much more natural and relatable presentation that also served to break up the monotony of the show.

Content is important, but the people are what makes the content stand out. Personalize your content and involve the listener as an active participant in everything you write for the air.

-34-

HOLLYWOOD GOSSIP

Most every show talks about entertainment news in some fashion. The most common way of doing so is in a standardized feature at the same time each morning. The most effective way is to use a character, even if just a listener that you set up with your information, and position them as a Hollywood insider. It's also effective to have one of your lesser-used role players on the morning show present the material. Whichever method you use, it's important to personalize it. Make it uniquely yours, rather than a regurgitation of last night's ET.

If he's available in your market, Claude Knobler is great for both Hollywood Gossip and entertaining movie reviews. Call 310 815-8727

Of course, there are many ways to identify with movies and pop culture. One station I know of sends several listeners to the new movies that open every Friday, with free tickets. The listeners call on Monday morning and review the new stuff. It works because you can pick people in your demo, and have them tailor the review to our audience — like adding a parents guide to sex, violence and the like.

-35-

THE POWER OF ENTERTAINMENT NEWS

Every show should be talking about the celebrities in the news, whether it's in a regular feature or as a part of their normal banter. In LA, Rick Dees capitalizes on that city's thirst for celebrity gossip with "Dees Sleaze". In fact, the name "Dees Sleaze" is a perfect example of name bonding with a feature. It ties Rick Dees into the bit and creatively reminds listeners who they are listening to.

Consultant Walt Sabo points out that a study of listeners yielded the following information:

- Most people know that Monday Nite Nitro is wrestling, but they don't know where Tom Brokaw works.

- Nobody knew the name of the president of Mexico or prime minister of Canada, but they know that Jennifer Love Hewitt became a star on Party of Five and Mark McGwire plays for the Cardinals.

The audience's tastes and knowledge are neither dumb nor smart. They are *perfect*. The audience has common interests, tastes and concerns and if you can tap into their appetite for entertainment, you're that much better off. Entertain them by talking about your listeners' interests. Gossip and rumors about the biggest Hollywood stars is something that has universal interest.

The Lone Ranger mentality is dead. It's been replaced with the "Three Musketeers" approach. ALL FOR ONE, and ONE FOR ALL wins! Utilize your staff strengths. Use your resources to win as a team. Success is rarely all your own doing— and it is *never* irreversible. Too many personalities satisfy their own ego and try to dominate all the material. This attitude is *never* successful! If your morning show has characters who don't have the ability to participate, find new people! And be sure they are *interesting!*

Protect against the temptation to try and be too "cool". Most stations that try to be cool fail. Listeners are looking for something that will make a lasting impression in their lives. Your success depends on your ability to perform up to those expectations.

36-

BATTLE OF THE SEXES

C hances are, you've done, or are currently doing, Battle of the Sexes. In fact, several shows in your market have probably aired this benchmark feature at some point. It may be a classic, but it's still as fresh and interesting today as it ever was. This bit is a *proven winner.*

But just in case you've been working on Pluto for the last 15 years, and are unfamiliar with how it works, Battle of the Sexes is a simple feature/contest that involves a male contestant answering questions that most women would know (cosmetics, fashion, cooking, etc) and a female answering questions that a man would most likely know (auto repair, sports, etc). Each contestant takes a crack at three questions and whoever answers the most correctly, wins. If there's a tie, you can ask bonus questions until the tie is broken, or declare it a tie for the day and bring back the same contestants the next day. Most of the time, shows will ask the daily "winner" to come back the next day and compete against a new contestant.

The contest is simple, and it's effective. The biggest challenge you face is staying interested in it *yourself.* Usually, the air personalities tire of this bit long before listeners do.

There are hundreds of BOTS questions on the *Morning Radio* web site tjohnsonmedia.com

It isn't usually necessary to offer an incentive to the contestants for being on, but you might want to have a small gift (CD, movie tickets, etc) as a "thank you" for playing.

The drama is enhanced when your show keeps score each day to determine a monthly or quarterly "champion", and the losing sex pays off a "bet". If you do this, be creative with the payoff, and create an *event* with it. When/if you consider a payoff, think in terms of creating a public stunt!

Here are a couple of ideas:

If women win:
>Guys have to dress in drag and lead a parade through downtown area
>Guys have to perform typically female jobs for a week for the female members

If men win:
>Women have to dress in bikinis and do the weather on a billboard for a morning
>Women have to wash the guy's cars

There is an endless supply of questions for Battle Of The Sexes. In fact, there's even a Battle of the Sexes board game loaded with content. Many show prep services post questions on a weekly or even daily basis. If yours doesn't, or if you don't subscribe, network with other morning shows to trade questions they've used in exchange for some that you come up with on your show. Listeners are also a great source of question. Just ask them to fax or email their

One great thing about Battle of the Sexes is that it is eternally relevant. You'll never have to worry whether the bit itself hits your target.

suggestions for questions.

Here are some sample questions to get you started.   :

(For Men)
- Which soap opera takes place in Oakdale? (" As the World Turns"0
- What would you buy at lucy.com? (women's sports apparel)
- Who makes the Essentials hair care collection? (Pantene)
- According to dermatologists how often should women replace disposable razors? (After 1-3 shaves)
- What product says it gives you "A Lifetime of Beautiful Skin?" (Oil of Olay)
- What's going on if someone says you have elephant ankles? (Your pantyhose are bunching up)
- What Proctor & Gamble product promises "Great Face?" (Noxzema)
- What is Regis Philbin's wife's name? (Joy)
- What kind of makeup makes the eyelashes look longer? (mascara)
- In women's clothing, what is a pump? (low heeled shoe)

(For Women)
- Who makes the RAV 4? (Toyota)
- 350 cubic inches was the standard for most cars made by what car company? (Chevy).
- What's the nickname of the F-20 fighter? (Tigershark)
- In what magazine might you see a Graham Wilson

If, or when, you run out of Brain Busters, just search on-line or visit your local bookstore. There are hundreds of sources for this type of feature that can be adapted for your show!

cartoon? (Playboy)
- What is BMX short for? (Bicycle Motocross)
- What electronic store's slogan is "You've got questions, We've got answers?" (Radio Shack)
- You want to impress your boyfriend by telling when its time to change his oil. How often should he change it? (3000 miles)
- The movie "Brian's Song" is the true story of Brian Piccolo, a football player who dies of cancer. Who played Piccolo? (James Caan)
- In college football, what are you talking about when you talk about the coalition? (Bowls)
- What former Chicago bears linebacker has a college player award named after him? (Dick Butkus).

There are several variations to Battle of the Sexes, including the Generation Gap game, in which contestants of different eras answer questions from each other's time. It can be pretty funny to hear a 20 year-old woman trying to come up with the answer to the question "Who ran for president on the Smothers Brothers show in the 60s?" (Pat Paulsen). Or hearing a 50 year-old man attempting to name all of the members of 'Nsync. But none of the variations get the audience involved as deeply as the Battle of the Sexes. It's a tried and true classic, and it's as timeless as the differences between men and women!

Your content can become memorable when you attach a "hook" to your bits. It's not as simple as a clever name. Often, meaningless but rhythmic word combinations become a powerful "hook" that listeners retain.

-37-

BRAIN BUSTERS

B rain Busters, or mind games, are popular ice breakers at some parties, and the riddles usually engage the participants in a mental exercise that you can exploit on the air. It's virtually guaranteed to create some phone action immediately, and it's easy to fit into any show. You can fit it in as a "throw away" over one break, or stretch it out for three or four, depending on how much time you have and how much attention you want to give to it.

You simply ask the question, repeat it, and solicit answers. The bit usually works best when you record phone calls and play them back in the order you want. This way, you can control how soon you get a winner and end the segment.

Here are some examples.
- Frank was bragging about his church's baseball team. He said, "Three of our four players hit homeruns and two of those homeruns were hit with the bases loaded. Our guys won 9 to 0 and not a single man crossed home plate." How is this possible? (they were all married)

- Jack stared through the dirty soot-smeared window on the 34th floor of the office skyscraper. Overcome with depression, he slid the window open and jumped through it. It was a sheer drop outside the building to the ground. Miraculously, after he landed he was completely unhurt. Since there was nothing to cushion his fall or slow his descent, how could he have survived? (Jack was so sick of window washing, that he opened the window and jumped inside!)

- Gary, the politician, was very tired after a long day of campaigning. He went to bed at 10pm, wound his alarm clock and set it for noon the next day. Since Gary fell asleep almost immediately, how many hours of sleep did he get before the alarm woke him up? (Two hours. Wind up clocks can't be set more than 12 hours in advance because they don't have AM and PM.)

- (Night jock) left the (radio station) and walked toward the parking lot. Without the benefit of moonlight or any artificial light, he was able to spot his black car 100 yards away. How was this possible? (it was daylight)

- Picture two plastic jugs filled with water. How could you put all of this water into a barrel, without adding the jugs or any divider to the barrel, and still be able to tell which water came from which barrel? (Freeze the water in one or both of the jugs, then cut the plastic away from ice)

- Officer Sam surveyed the scene, Sheik, the famous oil tycoon, was found shot to death while sitting in his car. The officer was puzzled by the fact that he couldn't find a single trace of gunpowder anywhere in the car. This led the officer to believe that Shiek had been murdered

Hundreds of questions are on-line at tjohnsonmedia.com

by someone outside the car. The strangest part is, all the windows and doors were completely closed and locked. The only bullet holes found were on Shiek's body. Since the car wasn't damaged, how did the assassin manage to kill him? (Shiek was in a convertible car)

- Farmer Brown came to town with some watermelons. He sold half of them plus half a melon, and found that he had one whole melon left. How many melons did he take to town? He took 3 melons to town.

Be sure you name your feature, to increase the chances of listener retention. There are too many messages competing for consumer's attention, and only so much room in the mind for recall.

-38-

LIE LIKE A GUY/WHINE LIKE A WOMAN

These two features are cousins, though "Lie Like A Guy" is usually far and away the most powerful feature. You're always better off bashing men than women. In fact, a good rule of thumb for many morning shows is that the "girl always wins".

"Lie Like A Guy" is a great feature in which you create a scenario that could easily happen to anyone. You then solicit women to call in and "lie" the way they would expect a guy to lie if the guy were in that sticky situation. It can be hilarious, create tension and controversy on the show, and usually results in some good old fashioned guy bashing. It is generally playful and good, innocent fun on the air. Perfect for female-targeted stations!

Here are some scenarios to get you started. It's easy to come up with more of your own, and many popular board games are loaded with ideas that can be adapted for an endless supply.

- You and your wife are eating a late dinner and listening to the radio. You hear the disc jockey talking with a lady on the phone. She wants to dedicate a song to her

CPA, Bill Gullicks. You are the only Bill Gullicks in town and you are a CPA... and dedicates "Secret Lovers" by Atlantic Starr! Your wife hears all of it and starts to turn white. Now, lie like a guy.

- You decide to surprise your husband by flying out to his business meeting to spend time with him. When you get to his hotel room a female co-worker of his answers the door wearing nothing but the shirt you gave him last Christmas. Now lie like a guy.

- You and your wife are about to make love. She watches you open a fresh box of a dozen condoms and put one one. Two weeks later you're about to make love again, she reaches for the condom box in the night stand only to find it empty. She knows the two of you have only made love maybe three or four times since you started the new box. She wants to know what happened to the missing condoms. Now, lie like a guy!

Whine Like a Woman is the flip side. If you're on a male-targeted station and don't care about those female numbers, you might want to go with it. Here are a few examples to consider:

- Your husband leaves a Snickers bar in his pants pocket. You find it after it ruins a whole load of laundry. Now whine like a woman.

- Your husband says he'll fix the oven before Sunday when your parents come over for dinner. He forgets and you find out an hour before your mom and dad arrive. It's too late to fix the oven. Now, whine like a woman.

- It's your anniversary. He gets front row tickets for the Bulls/Lakers. He says he's going and you can celebrate your anniversary tomorrow night. Now, whine like a woman.

- You're husband comes home and tells you that the two of you have been invited out with your boss for dinner tonight. You're not even close to presentable. You have no panty hose, your hair is a mess but he insists that you have to go and be a "good corporate wife." Now, whine like a woman.

-39-

QUESTION OF THE DAY

The Question Of the Day/Topic of the Day is easy to execute, and generally elicits terrific response from your listeners. However, the key to making it work best to your advantage is your ability to get into the question creatively, naturally and easily.

Too many shows just throw out the topic: "Okay, now it's time to call in and answer this question". While this approach may work, it does nothing to further your personality or develop character for the personalities or the show. This is an example of a lazy show taking the easy way out, or only going half-way in the show prep process.

A better way to showcase this feature is to tell a story that leads into the question. Use your *listeners* to call in and tell you a story that gets into the topic. Or have one of the members of the show talk about themselves, their "friends" or "family members" that lead into the topic. Be creative. Brainstorm natural ways to sound spontaneous. It takes a lot of work to prepare properly. *or, more accurately, our database of "ringers"*

Here are some questions to help get you started. Another great source of questions to get the phones ringing, and develop the personality of your air talent, is "The Book Of Questions".

- How many red flags does it take before you know your mate is cheating?

- Does your man love women with very big breasts?

- Has Mr. Right gone wrong?

- Weird doctor's office stories?

- Home improvement nightmares?

- How does your mate snore?

- How to get out of jury duty?

- Read the quotes of your high school yearbook?

- Do you treat your pet as if it were a member of the family?

- What's worse a man who can fix things and won't, or a man who can't fix things?

- Ever have a job you think was bad for your health?

- Does a 14-year-old girl have any business dating an 18-year-old guy? What if it were the other way around?

- How you got revenge on the boss?

- Women, your first bra experience (first trip to the store, first stuffing)? Every female can relate to this.

- Tell us about your nearest brush with fame...close celebrity encounters.

- You are at a friend's house enjoying a nice relaxing barbecue and you notice a cockroach in the salad. Would you say anything or keep quiet?

- Would you be willing to reduce your life by 5 years just to become the most attractive person in the world?

-40-

WORD FEATURES

There are many different bits you can do using the English language. One is the Word Of The Day. Create a character that drops in each day to "educate" your listeners on a new word. It could be a redneck, ethnic character, one of your interns, or someone from a neighboring state or community you like to poke fun at.

Sure it may be politically incorrect, but if you do it with a "caller" you should be able to get away with it! That character gives the word and an incorrect definition each day. It's simple and quick, but one of those features that gets listeners repeating it to their friends throughout the day. Be sure to post the entire "dictionary" on your web site with a photo of the character that delivers the "Word of the Day". Some examples follow.

> CHART: Since CHART goin', kin I use your concert tickets tomorrow night?

> VITAMIN. Couldn't filast night lookin' for my mama. She said Darnell, VITAMIN.

Find a full database of word games and ideas at tjohnsonmedia.com

-41-

WILL YOU LIE FOR ME?

A good weekly feature, or one of those that you can keep in your "arsenal" to pull out for occasional, regular, but unscheduled segments on the air. It's a simple concept that creates a feeling of discomfort as the listener participates vicariously through your 'contestant'.

First, find a listener willing to be on the phone, and conferenced with their mom, grandmother, etc. You provide a scenario with the listener that ends in them asking their mom to lie for them. For example:

"I'm in a job interview and this job is really important to me. They want to talk to you as a reference for me. When they call, they might ask about some things like the time I won the state spelling contest, and the time I donated a kidney to my step-sister so she could live, and how I graduated with honors from Duke University, and how I was a stripper during college to pay my own way through. Will you help me out?

Disclaimer/warning: Please observe your company's policy regarding privacy issues when making any calls to listeners. Federal law requires that when making outgoing phone calls, you obtain permission to air an individual's voice prior to putting them on the air.

-42-

Men Are Scum Day

This is a home run for any female-targeted show. Just open the phones for "What has happened to you that proves that "men are scum?" Just put women on to tell their story about their personal experiences. It's a perfect bit to thread throughout the entire show on the same day each week.

You may need to "prime the pump" for a week or two, but eventually the bit catches on and you'll have calls all morning. Do it once a week or once a month. It's a winner!

Many board games can be adapted to play on the air easily. Get Family Feud, Tri-Bond, etc. and mold them to fit your show.

-43-

USELESS TRIVIA

There are hundreds of sources of totally useless trivia, some of it interesting, but most of it has no impact on daily human life. How do you get that material on the air? Create a feature that showcases one of the personalities on the show in "character".

One method is to toss out 4-6 pieces of useless information at a time. In and of themselves, the items are mundane, and not that interesting. Collectively, and staged a properly, they can create a source of character-building dialogue between show members.

For example, the rest of the show can react to each item with responses that are appropriate to the character and/or to the item that is presented (amazement, interest, humor, disbelief, groan, challenge, etc).

An alternative would be to solicit a listener as a contestant. Read them five statements. They have to evaluate whether or not each statement is true or false. If they get at least three correct, they win a small prize.

Here are a few examples:

- If you toss a penny 10000 times, it will not be heads

5000 times, but more like 4950. The heads picture weighs more, so it ends up on the bottom.

- The glue on Israeli postage stamps is certified kosher.
- The longest word in the English language, according to the Oxford English Dictionary, is pneumonoultramicroscopicsilicovolcanoconiosis. The only other word with the same amount of letters is pneumonoultramicroscopicsilicovolcanoconioses, its plural. Hydroxydesoxycorticosterone and hydroxydeoxycorticosterones are the largest anagrams.
- Los Angeles's full name is "El Pueblo de Nuestra Senora la Reina de los Angeles de Porciuncula."
- Only one person in two billion will live to be 116 or older
- An ostrich's eye is bigger than it's brain.
- Ben and Jerry's send the waste from making ice cream to local pig farmers to use as feed. Pigs love the stuff, except for one flavor: Mint Oreo.
- Al Capone's business card said he was a used furniture dealer.
- The longest recorded flight of a chicken is thirteen seconds.
- Wilma Flintstone's maiden name was Wilma Slaghoopal,

You can do the same thing with headlines from newspapers. Here are some actual newspaper headlines that could be considered mistakes. They bring a smile, but are basically useless. Putting them in the proper context on the air can make them valuable:

- Grandmother of eight makes hole in one
- Deaf mute gets new hearing in killing

- Police begin campaign to run down jaywalkers
- House passes gas tax onto senate
- Stiff opposition expected to casketless funeral plan
- Two convicts evade noose, jury hung
- William Kelly was fed secretary
- Milk drinkers are turning to powder
- Safety experts say school bus passengers should be belted
- Quarter of a million Chinese live on water
- Farmer bill dies in house
- Iraqi head seeks arms
- Queen Mary having bottom scraped
- Is there a ring of debris around Uranus?
- Prostitutes appeal to Pope
- Panda mating fails - veterinarian takes over
- NJ judge to rule on nude beach

-44-

Your Mama Joke Off

I'm always impressed with personalities who are able to take a common, typical element and turn them into dynamic, memorable content. Everyone's heard dozens of "yo mama" jokes. (You know the ones...Yo' mama's so fat that when she sits around the house, she sits around the house). Funny jokes, but you can't just read them on the air. They have to be staged properly and put into context. Jeff & Jer brought this bit to life when they found a 16-year old kid who calls and exchanges the insults with Jerry. The rest of the show votes after each exchange on who had the best insult to the other's mama. Funny jokes...but only when put into the proper forum do they work on the air. Brilliant!

- Your mama is so fat she wakes up in sections.

- Your mama's teeth are so yellow that she spits butter.

- Your mama is so fat she plays hopscotch like this: New York, Miami, Chicago, Houston, Los Angeles.

- Yo Mama's so ugly, she could be a poster child for the burn center.

- Yo Mama's so ugly, she could make K.D. Lang go straight.

-45-

WOULD YOU RATHER

This is an interesting bit that can be a recurring theme on your show. It's simply asking listeners and show members which they would prefer…it can lead to some great discussions. You can also get some production elements from the movie "So I Married An Axe Murderer"

- First date nightmare: Would you rather have the worst hair day of all time or notice toilet paper trailing from your heel at the very end of the date?

- Would you rather spend the night with a dead boy in bed next to you, or share a cross country taxi ride with your worst enemy?

- Would you rather have to sleep each night between the mattress and box spring or only be allowed to listen to one piece of music the rest of your life, "My Heart Will Go On" by Celine Dion?

- Would you rather be awakened every morning by a special alarm clock that pours a bucket of cold water on your head or, always has to wear shoes that were one size too small?

- Would you rather find out that your grandfather owned slaves or find out he was a guard at a Nazi concentration camp?

-46-

"TIME WARP"

Flashing back to a prior year is perfect for any station that plays older music, or targets an audience over age 25.

However, if you are a contemporary station, you have to be careful to avoid making the show and station sound nostalgic. This bit works well at the same time each morning and is great for getting the non-participating audience playing along with your active audience. It's also a creative way to use those "Today in History" or "Today's Birthdays" elements in your show prep that may be interesting information, but difficult to put on the air.

Similar to the feature seen on the TV news program DATELINE (ABC), execute the bit with appropriate sound effects and production elements. Going into a stop set, you list several things that happened in a particular year. Coming out of the stop set, give a quick recap of the hints, then take calls from listeners guessing the year it happened (be sure to take calls in the particular order so that the *first* call does not get it correct). Or, if you don't want to turn it into a contest, you can simply give the answer coming out of the break. Then, play a song from that year. It's also a great way to get into a morning "flashback" song. Here are some examples:

- Evil Knievel fails in his attempt to rocket across the Snake River Canyon in Twin Falls, Idaho.
- In sports, the Oakland A's win their third consecutive World Series championship by beating the Dodgers.
- At the theatres, Ellen Burstyn won a Best Actress Oscar for "Alice Doesn't Live Here Anymore."
- And... on the record charts, "Rikki Don't Lose That Number" finds the number 4 postition for Steely Dan.

What year was it? 1973, 1974 or 1975?

Answer: "If you guessed 1974, you were right!"

- An episode of "Miami Vice" starred singer Phil Collins as a con man.
- Playboy shuts down the last three of it's "bunny" clubs owned by Playboy Enterprises.
- Burger King's new ad campaign featured a nerd, Herb, who's never eaten one of their burgers.
- Kate Smith, popular singer of "God Bless America," dies at age 79.
- And in sports, 20-year-old Mike Tyson becomes the youngest heavyweight boxing champion ever.

What year was it? 1986, 1987 or 1988?

Answer: "If you guessed 1986, you were right!"

- The series "The Love Boat" sets sail on her maiden voyage on ABC.
- Edward Koch is elected mayor of New York City for the first time.
- "Roots," airing for eight consecutive nights, becomes one of the most widely watched shows on TV.
- And, on the record charts, the "Rocky" theme ("Gonna

Fly Now") soars all the way to #1.

What year was it? 1976, 1977 or 1988?

Answer: "If you guessed 1977, you were right."

- A car driven by Senator Edward Kennedy plunges into the water on Chappaquiddick Island, Massachusetts,
- The U.S. holds the first military draft lottery since 1942.
- CBS cancels "The Smothers Brothers," who are too anti-war and anti-establishment for prime time.
- And... the Rolling Stones performed at Altamont where a fan is killed, allegedly by a Hell's Angel.

What year was it? 1967, 1968 or 1969?

Answer: "If you guessed 1969, you were right!"

-47-

Fact Or Fiction/Truth or Lie

This is a simple feature that is easy to execute, interactive and perfect for that material you just don't know what to do with. Just get a caller on the phone and read some statements to them. It can be current events, trivia or just about anything. The caller has to identify whether the statement is true or not. Get three out of five correct to win!

-48-

KIDS FAMILY SECRETS

T his is a great feature to recycle on a regular basis. Once a month or so works great. You ask kids to call in. Bribe them tell you a secret that they've been told to never tell anyone. You'll get some incredible stories on the air! Art Linkletter made a career out of talking to kids, and this is a perfect forum to do the same.

There are five topics you can talk about on the air and *never* go wrong: Kids, sex, pets, money and relationships. They all represent topics that create passion, emotion, and strong opinions.

-49-

TRIVIA MAN/SLAYING THE "BEAST"

Trivia is always tempting, but on most shows it turns into a long, boring segment that fails to mean anything. It's...well, trivial! However, there are ways to turn those little-known facts into compelling elements that entertain!

One way is to turn one of the characters on your show into "useless trivia man". He or she delivers those factoids in sequence.

Jeff & Jer occasionally do a great trivia segment called "Slaying the Five-Headed Beast". Jerry asks five difficult trivia questions, each representing a "head" of the "beast". Listeners call and offer answers to all five questions simultaneously. Using a voice-changing processor, Jerry (as the "beast") responds with the number of heads the caller has killed. However, he does not indicate which questions they answered correctly. You can usually stretch this bit over a couple of days, and sometimes up to a week!

-50-

PRANK CALLS

P rank phone calls get tremendous reaction. Rick Dees created a benchmark with his "Candid Phone Calls". John Lander has used "Burn Your Buns" as a weapon in developing his legend. In fact, the masters of the prank call, The Jerky Boys, parlayed their skill into a movie a few years ago. Fortunately for morning shows, outgoing calls to unsuspecting victims plays much better on the air than on the silver screen!

If you are creative, fast on your feet, and have planned for any "detours" in your prank call, these can be tremendous features on your show. The tension and risk involved creates talk and word of mouth. What's more, it's the type of bit that your audience wants to hear again and again! They'll call and request a great prank call as if it were a hit song!

There are several keys to a great prank call:

1. Know where you are going. If it's going to work, you have to know what the punch line is before you start the call, and maintain a focus on where you intend to go with the call.

2. Practice! Role-play the prank call with other show members, or staff members before you

make the call. This will help you refrain from breaking into laughter as you set them up (it's always funnier the first time). It also will alert you to areas that may create problems for you.

3. Record the call. Don't try it live. Most prank calls take a long time to get to the punch line, and there is an excess of down time that is just not entertaining. Not only will you end up with a more entertaining call, you will insure that bad calls never make it to air.

4. Edit! Most prank calls take 15-20 minutes. By the time you edit out the "trash" your finished product will probably be under five minutes.

5. Inform the victim. One of the most entertaining parts of your prank call can be when you reveal your true identity, and capture the victim's response.

6. Don't be mean! It's just not funny to call someone and tell them that their husband has been killed in an accident. It's not creative and it's not in good taste. Listeners love it when you are playful, fun, and take some chances, but once you cross the line of what they consider "good taste", it's hard to get back in their good graces. Have fun with listeners, but be careful!

You can get an endless supply of prank call ideas from your audience. Ask them to give you the scenario for a prank on someone they know, and they *will* respond.

Unfortunately, many shows are no longer allowed to use this feature. If you plan to use prank calls in your repertoire, be sure you observe federal law and company policy. Fortunately, there are ways around the restrictions. First, arrange a network of personalities in other markets to play the role of victim. You can also set up friends and co-workers to help you out this way, but be careful to not tip off too many people inside the station. A disgruntled employee may pop off to the local newspaper and you risk being discredited.

There are a few new services that provide actors and actresses to be the "victims" for your calls.

PART 4: INTERVIEWS
INTERACTING WITH GUESTS AND
CELEBRITIES ON THE AIR

-51-

INTERVIEWS

At some point, interviews are a part of nearly every show. Whether it's a formal interview, an author, a celebrity or just and interesting listener, there will be times when you are in a position to ask questions one-on-one. Interviewing skills come naturally to some, but most personalities break out in a cold sweat whenever they are in a position to chat with someone famous.

Improving your interview skills start with your own attitude toward the interview. You simply *must* learn to relax and be comfortable with your interview. A lot of talented personalities tense up and become different people when their guest's microphone is turned on.

You should strive to become a market celebrity, not just a good air personality!

Do you *need* guests on your show? No. But if you don't, you're missing out on an opportunity to raise your profile with your audience. Listeners want to think of radio personalities as stars. When you have access to famous people, your image as being a "star" increases.

Interviewing a celebrity provides the opportunity to give your listener access to the stars that they could never obtain on their own. Sometimes, simply allow your listeners to interview the celebrity. You're the hero with the listener for being the conduit to making that happen!

-52-

HOW TO CONDUCT INTERESTING INTERVIEWS

Securing a celebrity or compelling person on the air is often difficult, but not nearly as difficult as turning the guest appearance into an interesting segment on the air. The truth is, there are not many personalities with great, or even good, interview skills.

Study the habits of effective interviewers. Barbara Walters, for example, has the ability to elicit honest, emotional responses from her subjects because she asks difficult questions with empathy and compassion. Her brilliance is constructing questions that are very personal, very poignant, without being considered rude or intrusive. Her talent is making the guest feel comfortable with her, that she is their friend. That breaks down the barriers and gets them to open up.

Larry King is a terrific interviewer, but is effective for very different reasons. Larry's policy is to ask questions his listeners and viewers would likely ask. To help him do this, he makes it a point to avoid over-preparation. He always has the background on his subject, but does not read the book before interviewing the author.

If you can't get a celebrity to come on the show, use your imagination. Some personalities claim that the celebrity was booked for an interview, and stood you up. Then, set up an answering machine, and let listeners call and leave (celebrity) a message instead. Play back some of the messages on the air.

In all of your interviews, never ask the expected questions. Like Larry King, ask "real people" questions. There is nothing more boring than hearing a DJ ask an entertainer "How did you get your start?" or "Whose music influenced you when you were starting out?". Nobody cares, but it's common to use these "fall back" questions to cover poor interviewing techniques.

It helps to solicit the assistance of your friends or family to come up with a list of 20-30 questions about any celebrity. Use those. They're more likely to be things your audience is truly interested in, rather than the mundane, routine and expected questions.

It also helps to consider the interviewee as more than someone to simply conduct a question and answer session. Consider them to be guests *on* your show, not *of* your show. That's an important distinction. If they're a guest *on* your show, you'll involve them in all of the features and entertainment elements your listener is accustomed to. It makes it much more interesting for your guest, and therefore, more likely to be a successful segment.

Another tactic is to find out other morning shows the guest has been on recently and network with those shows or producers to find out what worked well, and what didn't. It might even be worthwhile to ask the guest (or their publicity people) what has been a "winner" in other recent interviews. This will not lead to your best material, of course, but will give you an indication of a direction to take.

Celebrity guests will always be late for your interview appointment. Plan accordingly!

-53-

HELPING GUESTS OPEN UP

For most celebrities, a large part of their time is spent dealing with media, and after being bombarded with the same questions day after day, they become robotic in their responses. Not only that, most of the time they've been coached to respond in a certain way to the expected questions. So your first task is to take them out of that element and make them feel more comfortable.

What's more, your guest will be more likely to take an interest in the discussion and really open up to you. When you get them away from the standard Q & A, they become more human, more "real" to your listeners.

Here are just a few questions to help get you out of the routine:

- Who are some of your heroes?
- Who do you look up to personally?
- What book is on your night table right now?
- If you had a day to spend any way you want, just for yourself, what would you do?
- If we were to ride together to lunch in your car, what music would be playing in your CD player?
- What is it you would like people to admire about

you?
- If you could be anyone you wanted to be, who would it be and why?
- How do you handle stress?
- What was your last "regular" job before you made it big?

Make them feel comfortable and make them more human to your listeners. Anything that causes the audience to relate to a celebrity will hook them on the interview. If you can make a personal connection between your show and the celebrity, your audience will participate vicariously through you. So think of ways you can make the interview more personal. If you have more than one or two people in the room, make sure everyone on your staff is wearing a tag with their name on it. It will help them connect with you if they call you by your name.

Ask about their golf game, their kids, their family, their successes and failures. Ask a musical guest if they've ever been forced to record a song that they really didn't LIKE. These make more interesting, and often more inspiring, stories.

If your guest is boring you, you're boring your listeners. Get rid of them! You were probably brought up to be polite and sensitive to the feelings of others, but that has no place when you're interviewing a guest.

Most of the time, people you interview don't have very good micro-phone skills. They stand too far away from the mike. Be sure to have someone on your staff assigned the task of moving the micro-phone into position, without being rude to your guest.

-54-

TAKING CHANCES

So what happens when you have a great guest, but he or she is surrounded by controversy or is involved in something sensitive? Simple. You *must* find a way to talk about it on the air. Your audience will respect you if you do, and you'll lose their trust if you don't.

A few years ago, Bert Weiss, producer of Mix 107's Diamond in the Morning show in Washington DC, told a story about an interview with Jackson Browne. Browne was on a typical promotional tour to hype his new album, and his "handlers" had told Bert and Jack Diamond that they could ask anything they wanted, *except* they had to stay away from the issue of Darryl Hannah. Apparently, Browne walked out of an interview the day before when he was asked about his alleged physical abuse of Hannah.

After a few minutes of "warm up", Diamond decided to push it. He asked, "Jackson, do you mind if we get personal for a second?" Browne responded by saying, "Not really. If I don't like your question, I just won't answer it." So, as Bert relates the story,

"Jack, very softly and politely, asks, 'What happened with Darryl?'. You could hear a pin drop in the

Talk Host Phil Hendrie describes what it takes to become successful as a unique air talent: "Be fearless and re-spectful. You have to try any-thing and every-thing. Be who you are on the Radio.

studio. Complete silence. I didn't know if Jackson was going to walk out or Jack was just going to go to spots because there is just nothing but complete silence for 15 seconds. No lie...15 seconds! Finally, Jackson glances around the room for some help, then looks right at Jack and says, 'She lied! She just out and out lied, Jack'. He then talked candidly and openly about their entire relationship for several more minutes.

Why did Diamond take the risk and ask the question? He said that it was the *one* question that everyone listening wanted answered. The listeners would have been disappointed if he didn't ask it.

When preparing for an interview, plan your questions carefully so you go into interviews with the intent of asking questions that might lead to answers that will make the news. Think in terms of how you can get local or national coverage with what you ask. That's a tall order, but if youprepare along these lines, your much more likely to elicit a more compelling response.

From The Desk Of...Francisco T. Escaraio

"There is a fine line between bravery and stupidity. If you get away with it, you are brave. If   not,

---

Play to WIN...*instead of playing* NOT to LOSE.

-55-

IMPROVE YOUR CHANCE FOR A SUCCESSFUL INTERVIEW

Some personalities are naturally good interviewers. Some are horrible, and no matter how much they work at it, they just can't get it right. After all, just like in a relationship, you just can't change the person more than 5 or 10%. For most, though, interview skills can be improved and can be a useful weapon in the morning show arsenal. *Preparation* is key to all successful interviews. Now, most personalities know the subject matter well enough, and have studied the material in enough depth to have the knowledge it takes to interview their subject, but too often their preparation is too surface, too generic. It lacks the depth to get to more than just the typical questions and answers. There's no *impact*. How many times have you heard a celebrity asked, "Who was your biggest influence?" BORING!!!!

Preparation: The first step in building a successful element on the air. The other two steps are concentration and moderation. You cannot take short cuts in the preparation phase.

In FMQB magazine, consultant Pat Welsh (Pollack Media Group) offers some more guidelines for insuring that your interviews will become more dynamic and exciting than your competitor:

1. **Do your homework:** Learn enough about your

See *Morning Radio I* --Chapter 7

guest to avoid embarrassment. There's nothing worse than asking a question about a project, only to find out that the subject was not involved!

2. **Look for help:** Research your material well. Scan the internet, contact publicists, go to the library. Find out all you can about your guest. That familiarity will lead to a confidence and comfort zone when the interview is underway.

3. **Think like a listener:** Just like Larry King conducts all his interviews from the audience's perspective! Get away from the "where are you going next" type questions. Nobody really cares. Instead, ask about their best and worst experiences on the road. How do you achieve this? Practice it! Better yet, ask friends, relatives and associates what they would like to know about the interviewee.

4. **Get your guests to arrive early:** The more comfortable they are with your studio, your people and your environment, the better.

5. **Let THEM be the "star":** Your job is to make them sound interesting. Don't try to upstage them. You're the "straight" man.

6. **Know the answers before you ask the question:** A good lawyer doesn't ask questions they don't already know the answer to. If you've done your homework, you should know just about everything that your audience doesn't. TV talk show hosts use

When a celebrity is on your show, have a list of things you can have them record for future use. Not just a "This is/you're listening to" but meaningful lines that can be used regularly. Have them introduce your show features and show elements (news, traffic, etc.). Ask them to do a show introduction or "good-bye", or say "Happy Holidays" or "Happy Thanksgiving". You'll only use them once a year, but they'll sound fresh and unique each time you do.

screeners to do pre-interviews to make sure the conversation goes in a positive way, eliminating questions that will be less interesting!

7. **Don't answer your own questions:** One of the most common mistakes is leaving the guest with nothing more than a "yes or no" answer. Make sure your questions are brief, clear and lead to a longer, detailed response. How many times have you heard an interview consist mostly of the personality making statements, leaving the guest to respond, "yeah that's right".

8. **Put the person in a new light:** Find a way to make the guest more human. Ask them about things that are happening in the world. Ask athletes to rate recent movies or music. Ask movie stars what sports teams they follow.

9. **Do constant re-sets:** No matter how famous your guest is, you still have listeners who don't know who they are. Listeners tune in and out all the time, and it's important to re-introduce your guest frequently. In fact, every couple of minutes is not too often. This applies to the entire show!

10. **Have a backup plan:** Have a list of questions that you can pull out in case the interview slows down.

Why is it so hard for people to realize that winners work harder, prepare better, and generally perform at a higher level as a result of their dedication?

56-

TAKING AN ANGLE

O ne of the most important things you can do in the interview is consider it an opportunity to stand out, and create a newsworthy event in the interview! It's not just a chance to have a celebrity on, but an opportunity to find out something that local media, and even the national press, would find interesting.

When Fox TV's special "Who Wants To Marry A Millionaire" created a controversy over Rick Rockwell's marriage to Darva Conger, Jeff & Jer were able to secure Rockwell for a private and exclusive interview. In the aftermath of the TV show, nearly all of the attention on Rockwell was negative. It would have been easy for Jeff & Jer to "pile on", put Rockwell on the air and let listeners unload. But would it have been newsworthy?

Instead, the show brought him in with an open mind and asked listeners to consider his side of the story. They treated him with fairness, compassion and interest. Not only did Rockwell tell his story with emotion and sincerity, he changed Jeff & Jer's minds about him. The result: A story that was covered on all local television

stations and several national programs! It all happened because Jeff & Jer took a different, unique approach that had not yet been considered!

It is risky. It's hard. It takes nerve. You will be ouside your comfort zone. Take the risk and try it. It's what it takes to be successful! And when (not *if* but *when*) you fail, forget about it, move on and try again.

Whenever you interview a celebrity, think outside the box. What has the subject not been asked yet? What angle has not yet been explored? How can your show be unique and *different?*

Are you prepared to do whatever it takes to be successful? Do you believe in yourself, your abilities and have the courage to be uniquely yourself? Are you willing to do things differently and take risks?

From The Desk Of...Brad Gilbert

"When you beat up on yourself during a match, you've doubled the number of people trying to defeat you."

-Brad Gilbert is America's #1 tennis coach

-57-

WHO TO INTERVIEW?

If you decide to book guests, you can fill up your show with them. Everybody has something to share with the world. But relatively few deserve any time on your show. Why? The audience just doesn't *care*.

Whenever you consider having a guest on the show, you have to ask the question, "Who cares"? Who will this interview or guest attract to our station or show? Will they tell their friends about it? Will this guest attract media coverage? Does anybody really care?

Authors are always available, and usually make for some really *boring* interviews. Why have them on? They write books! People *read* books. Very few authors make for good radio. The exception, of course, is a celebrity who is pushing a book. You may have to let them talk about their book to get them on the show to talk about what *is* interesting.

Record companies often provide their up and coming recording artists, but how often are those artists popular with your listeners? Usually, they are clutter. There are some artists who are so entertaining they are worth having on. They're *fun*. But most are just clutter! Who cares?

wan

Interviews are hard work. The good ones are hard to gete, because *everybody* wants them.

I hear the excuses all the time: "I could do great interviews too, if I was able to get good celebrities. That's no excuse. It's a cop-out. Get out there and work to improve the quality of guests on your show. And don't use your lack of resources as an excuse for boring interviews. It's too easy to complain about things we don't have instead of using the things we do.

Whenever you have a guest on the show, it's important to make them feel comfortable as quickly as possible. Relate to them with "every day" questions that you would ask a friend, such as, "Where did you go to school?", "Who did you vote for?" "What do you want for Christmas?" In fact, you should have a list of these questions nearby and use them regularly, not just for guests but for listeners calling in to contribute to the show. They're great icebreakers and show your audience that you relate and care about the person on the phone. And, since each caller is a surrogate for the entire audience, it will translate that you care about your listeners, too.

PART 5: PROMOTING THE SHOW

USING ALL RESOURCES TO CREATE PUBLICITY

-58-

Promoting Your Show on Air

How would you like to have your show promoted to a 15%-20% of your market each day, every day, around the clock? Your message to "listen to WXXX for the (your name) morning show would air 6-12 times per day. Not only that, but the message would be delivered in the midst of the most high profile programming, and never "buried" between other messages. How much is that worth to you? You couldn't afford it. Your station could never come close to purchasing a marketing campaign that powerful.

If your station airs a promo campaign (and if they don't, you should be asking "why not"), you have a tremendous tool at your disposal. Listeners to your station are likely to be candidates to become fans of your morning show.

Still, I have heard a lot of complaints-yes, *complaints*-from morning shows that are burdened with the task of producing those daily morning show promos. It's as if they are being commanded to take out the garbage, or have lunch with a client. Do you have any idea how valuable that air time is?

How important this opportunity is to build the *brand* and

image of your character and personality? It's priceless. Stop complaining. Keep those promos fresh, new and exciting!

As a general rule, promos are more effective if they play audio from a previous show, demonstrating the personality of the show, than pre-promoting what is coming up tomorrow. Use your promo slots to image your show. Count on your compelling personality to convert those listeners into partisans.

-59-

THE PURPOSE OF PROMOS

Now that you're convinced promos are a good idea, how do you create promos that actually *work?* How can you produce great new promos that capture the flavor of your show, and leave the audience with the desired impression? More importantly, how can you increase the chances that your promos will influence listener behavior?

First, understand that it is very difficult to convince listeners to change their habits. Just because you say something doesn't mean anyone is paying attention. Even if you repeat it a million times, will you convince someone to listen at a time that doesn't fit into their schedule? Of course not.

Merely offering "a lot of music without a lot of talk" or "more fun tomorrow morning to get you going" isn't enough incentive to motivate an audience to tune you in.

Promos should show off the personality, performance and mood that you project in your show and in your station. Your content is irrelevant. It's the emotion that cuts through. Clever, original promos that make a statement about the show will, over time, increase your chances of attracting a larger, and more attentive audience.

-60-

PRINCIPLES OF GREAT PROMOS

One thought. Remember those instructions from your first job in radio? You were ordered to construct your breaks with only one thought per break! Guess what? That first program director was right! He may not have known why, but his idea was correct. It's true that listeners only take one thought from any of your messages. Not only does this apply to the content on your show, it is even more true as it pertains to promos.

"Concentration of force" applies here. Never give your audience more than they can absorb.

Few words. Your promos should be written and produced to establish a mood, and create an image for your show. Demonstrate the desired sound that represents your intended show image. You do that with *sound* and not with a large quantity of words. Your words should be carefully chosen to drive your message, but avoid the temptation of trying to use long verbage to drive your message home.

Include your audience. Find ways to demonstrate how your show can enhance the life of your listener. Show them

See "Repetition Works" for details on the principle of Concentration of Force" in Chapter 5 of *Morning Radio 1*

the benefits of listening. Spend less time writing copy that explains *why* you are better, and more time demonstrating how your show fits into your audience's lifestyle.

Be real, and communicate honestly. Your message should be delivered naturally and with contained excitement. Enthusiasm is a good word here. Enthusiastic promos are exciting. Excited reads are frantic. Low-key the presentation. Listeners will reject the fake, insincere sound of those old "announcers". They *relate* to warm human beings. When you over-sell your message, listener defense mechanisms are activated and the listener is turned off.

Write powerfully. Sell softly. In fact, don't *sell* at all. Your copy should offer suggestions to impact the decision of who your audience should choose to listen to. Over time you will persuade them to make the right choice. If the words pack a punch, you don't need to exaggerate the "read".

Be accessible. Your promo will cut through by being non-threatening. If your promo comes across with an in-your-face demand to listen, your audience's guard goes up, and you won't influence them. They tune you out, and the promo becomes clutter.

Use humor. Your listeners like to laugh. But be sure it's funny! The key to funny promos is funny writing. And remember, if it's not funny on paper, it won't be funny on the air. Nothing bombs like a comedian that gets no laughs. Promos are even worse!

At Star 100.7/San Diego, we run a promo for Jeff & Jer's 10pm-2am "Replay" that says, "The Jeff & Jer Replay...we're not that great, but it's about the only thing on." It's non-threatening, and self-deprecating enough to be effective.

Don't make commands. Offer suggestions. Instead of telling someone to "take action now", tell them a story about how to USE your station or show. A campaign featuring slice of life examples are usually effective. when you offer a promo with a set of instructions ("listen tomorrow", "tune in now", "don't miss it") are threatening to listeners. Soften your message when you "ask for the order" by using *coaxing* words instead of *command* words. Words like "you could", "you might" or "maybe it's for you" are much more likely to be effective in persuading listeners to sample you.

Let the listener sell. If you want to claim you're great, make sure it's a *listener* making that claim. Let them go out of the way congratulating you. Those spots that say how great you are aren't nearly as effective as those that feature a listener thanking you, or telling you how you have benefited their life. If *you* say it, it's *hype*. If *they* say it, it's believable and the message is much more likely to be received and believed!

Re-write, and re-edit. Keep your promos short. Keep them focused. Keep them powerful.

Paint mental pictures. Play on the emotions. Design your promo for drama. Pull your listeners into your promo and into your show to the point that they think they are part of your family! This is how you create the feeling that they will miss something if they don't listen. Have you noticed the messages used by TV networks the last few years? They're designed to promote a mood or image rather than

Hype: Frantic, over-promotion of an activity or event. Essential function of most advertising. However, success is measured by the benefits of hype without a trace of it's presence!

Until the people meter is in effect, Arbitron doesn't measure what people listen to. It measures what the sample remembers. One of the primary objectives for your promos is to help them remember when and to whom they are listening.

command you to watch. Statements like "You, me and ABC", "It's not TV, it's HBO" and "Welcome Home to CBS" convey a refreshinig method of positioning images

Avoid facts. That is not to suggest that you falsify the promos, but focus on selling the sizzle, not the steak. Facts are boring. Facts are details. Facts are great for newspaper inserts for grocery store ads. They aren't entertaining. Don't bog down your message with details.

Update your promo. Effective promos have a shelf life of about 18 hours, from the time you get off the air, until midnight that evening. After that, they are outdated, and should be scrapped. If you were paying for the air time your promo takes up, you'd make sure that there was always fresh copy! If you understand the value of a promo, failure to update promos is a basic sign of laziness.

Remember that your promos aren't just to persuade someone to try you for the first time. They won't bring new cume to your radio station. The only people who hear them are people who are already listening. However, they *can* recruit station listeners to try your morning show. They *can* stretch your time spent listening. Your promos *should* cause existing listeners to listen more. They *must* help listeners recall the station/show they are listening to already. They also serve the purpose of confirming that listeners have already chosen wisely in listening to you in the first place.

Promos are always stronger when they sell content. TV promos are always content-driven, and they are very effective. Your personality cannot be duplicated!

-61-

DRESS UP YOUR WORDS

When writing your promos, understand the strength of your words and how they impact your image. Many words are neutral and simply serve to set up more powerful words. Unfortunately, many station promos are almost exclusively composed of these type words. They leave out the impact words. Other times, stations load up a promo with so many action impact words that the promo becomes cluttered and confusing.

Instead, strive for combining a few powerful words to create a natural, positive response with your audience. In fact, if you study the advertising industry and how they exploit automatic internal responses to powerful words and emotions, your promos (and your show) will undergo dramatic change. Successful advertisers have learned how to use words to leverage you to take action.

In his book, "*In The Zone*", Dr. J. Mitchell Perry points out an example from a box of cereal: "Notice the words and phrases judiciously selected to appear on a box of Nabisco Shredded Wheat include *wholesome, pure, lightly toasted, 100% natural, crunchy biscuit, high quality, original, family, fresh, whole wheat* and *great taste.* Those words are chosen with care. Each has been weighed, analyzed, and measured as to its individual and

When choosing your words for promos, write in plain English. Avoid speaking in radio-ese. Sell benefits of your show and why your station should be their primary "button"

collective impact on you. Every single word is evocative. In fact, reading the list out of context should make you hungry for Shredded Wheat, which is exactly why they were chosen.....You'll notice words and phrases such as *dry, tastes like hay, flavorless,* and *expensive*are rarely printed on the side of a box of cereal, for the same reason. Those words are also (equally) evocataive, but experts know they will push you away from their product."

Your word selection also affects the way those words are delivered to your audience. Inflection, pace, tempo and other aspects of the "read" will convey emotion through the words.

Further, use positive words to describe your show. It seems like this should be obvious, but too many promos fail to cast a positive image over the product they are trying to describe.

This goes for your performance on the air, too. Your show will be much more successful if you train yourself to be positive, rather than using a negative, less enthusiastic vocabulary.

-62-

USE POSITIVE WORDS

When you write a promo, you are attempting to persuade, or coax a potential customer (listener) to take an action (listen to you) that they may or may not be inclined to do on their own.

What will be most successful in accomplishing this daunting task? Successful parents, coaches and maanagers are more effective in teaching or persuading their personnel when they motivate with positive words.

Which has a better chance of creating a positive action for you:

The Nike campaign of "Just Do It" is a perfect example of a powerful, positive ad campaign. They boldly challenge you to get out and get active!

From The Desk Of...Bill Walsh

"You demonstrate a lack of assuredness when you talk in negatives...always take a supportive approach rather than a negative approach."

       Bill Walsh is a legendary football coach, best known for his success with the San Francisco 49ers.

EXAMPLE 1:

"Let's pull together and give it 100% today. If we do, we'll go over the top and exceed our goal."

or,

"Let's pick it up and get moving here, people. We have to give it 100% or we're going to fall short."

EXAMPLE 2:
"If you don't get a B or better on the math test, you'll be grounded for a month."

or,

"Do the best you can, and if you get a B, we'll go to Disneyland to celebrate."

Would history have turned out differently if Richard Nixon had proclaimed "I am innocent" instead of "I am not a crook?" What if Bill Clinton had stated that "I am faithful to my wife" rather than "I did not have sex with that woman?"

Somewhere during the maturation process, human beings evolve into a species that encourages negative reactions through the language we speak.

Obviously, the positive message is a much more powerful statement for increasing performance. It's the same with your promos. Put everything in positive, constructive terms. Describing your show in terms that demonstrate why you *should* listen is much more persuasive than the threatening tones of *'Don't miss it"*.

Choose your words carefully to create a powerful image. Wouldn't you rather be around someone with a positive outlook than a negative one?

Do everything you can to become recognized and generate publicity, but don't let it get in the way of entertaining your audience. Word-of-mouth advertising about your show will yield tremendous results. If you can entertain and impress a listener on a deep, emotional level, you will be more successful than you can ever imagine. Persuading 100% of the available listening audience 10% of the way is no more effective than convincing 10% of the audience 100% of the way,

-63-

EXTERNAL VISIBILITY: CREATING A "BUZZ"

Getting out in public is a wonderful way to endear yourself to the audience. When you shake the hand of a listener, and tell them who you are, invite them to listen to you, they will! It's not a sure-fire guarantee of increased ratings, but it helps. Still, simply getting in people's faces isn't enough. In most markets, it's impossible to make enough appearances and shake enough hands to have a significant impact.

Still, street presence is good, but you must choose your appearances carefully. Not all outside appearances will make you look good. Handing out stickers on a street corner will gain you visibility, but not respect.

Not all appearances create goodwill. Be sure that when you appear in public, you delight your listener, surpassing all expectations. Leave them with an experience that exceeded anything they could have hoped for. Make them proud to have met you and anxious to brag to their friends that they "know" you. If you're giving away doughnuts, make sure there are enough doughnuts for *everyone* (and coffee and juice would be a nice touch, too).

Staying in front of the public is one requirement for your show to maintain any level of success. When do you stop making an impression in public? Never. When you have finally reached a level of market "star" you must work even harder to keep that edge! Michael Jordan became the greatest basketball player in history because he got the most out of his extraordinary talent with an unmatched work ethic. He never stopped practicing, never stopped shooting free throws after practice. That's the difference between outstanding performers and true superstars. When you achieve success in your market, work harder. Make more appearances. Shake more hands. Use your celebrity status as leverage to become larger than life!

Your looks can hurt you in public. Hey, maybe you have a great face for radio. Be honest with yourself and your strengths and weaknesses. If showing your face in public makes parents take children off the street, maybe you should stay off the street Looks really *do* matter. Through the magic of radio, listeners will create an image of you in their mind based on how you *sound* to them. If your public appearance disappoints them, that image will be tainted forever. You want people to *like* you, not feel sorry for you.

Wanna create a crowd, and a huge media event? Start with a great crowd. As P.T. Barnum once said, "Nothing draws a crowd like a crowd." Stage events where a natural audience already gathers.

Getting ratings is like campaigning to win an election that takes place in a listener's mind. You are constantly working to be "top of mind" and win the election. Your job is to raise awareness and win the popular vote!

-64-

MEDIA ACCESSIBILITY

Since the biggest reason to do a public relations stunt is to generate publicity, it's important to spend significant time *off* the air to increase the chances of gaining positive coverage and identification. After all, the only thing more disappointing than being ignored by the TV stations and newspapers is being referred to only as "a local radio station".

There's no way to guarantee coverage, but you can take some steps to increase your chances of seeing your stunt on the late news!

The first step is to make sure the television stations and newspapers know about the event. It seems like common sense, but too many stations send out a press release and then wonder why nobody came to cover the event. It's probably because the publicity never made it to the right person, and even if it did, it was of little importance to them. When contacting television stations, make sure you talk to the assignment editors for each shift, as well as the reporters. Personal contact will produce better results than faxing, mailing or emailing your press information. After all, what happens to press releases and requests for publicity at *your* station?

By the way, when working with the media, a little "schmoozing" goes a long way. If the assignment editor comes through for you, send them tickets to a concert or a movie. Take them to lunch. Do anything you can to establish a relationship and express your appreciation for the coverage they provide.

Make sure the personal contact comes from someone of significance. This isn't a job for an intern. Spend some time and invest some resources to increase your chances of coverage. If you're serious about obtaining coverage, you need to assign a trained professional to the task.

Invite reporters to participate with you. Especially if the stunt is to benefit a charity, challenge them to have a personal stake in your effort.

Most of all, think visually. Evaluate the site of the stunt the way the media is going to see it. What will be a convenient location for them to cover your event easily, and frequently? Be sure to save some parking for the reporters and camera crews you invite to your event, and tell them in advance exactly where they should park.
You want television coverage, so make it easy for the stations to cover your event. Provide them with all they need to make their job easier, thereby encouraging multiple exposures on their newscasts. Here are a few things to consider:

    1. Sight lines. When they shoot the video, what will the camera see? This is much different than what the public will see at the event, and

requires some attention.

2. Be sure your call letters are visible in every possible camera angle. TV reporters love to cover outrageous stories, but credit "a local radio station". Insuring that you logo is prominently displayed everywhere provides protection against this. It should be on all staff members' clothing (and it should be in current, contemporary fashions, not station t-shirts), microphones, contestant clothes (if any) and hats. Be sure banners surround the point of focus on all sides.

3. When interviewed for the media, be sure the call letters and your show name(s) are always mentioned frequently. When asked, "How did this crazy idea start?", your response should be something like, "On the WXXX morning show last week, the topic came up and....", or, "Well, (name) of the WXXX morning show had the original idea, and ...".

4. NAME the stunt/promotion something that includes the show name, personality name(s), or call letters.

Finally, remember that gaining publicity is work, and requires persistence. Don't give up. If they ignore you on the first call, call them back. Follow up. Getting coverage in the media will lead to increased top-of-mind awareness for you and your station, but it requires a well-orchestrated campaign. And, as you establish relationships with the right media personnel, your coverage will continue to grow

If you want to take it up a notch, help the camera crew by installing television lighting. You can switch them on whenever needed.

From The Desk Of...Jack Nicklaus

"I'm a firm believer in the theory that people only do their best at things they truly enjoy. It is difficult to excel at something you don't enjoy."

Jack Nicklaus, golfing legend.

-65-

SHAKING HANDS & KISSING BABIES

O ne of the most important goals you should have is to reach out and touch each listener (and each potential listener) on a personal level. Yet most personalities aren't nearly as "reachable" as they should be. Worse, when they *are* in public, they tend to hide from the listeners who seek them. You're more liikely to find them sitting in the van with a cool soft drink than working the crowd.

To win the ratings game, you have to win the election, much as if you are running a campaign. Politicians know that when they shake someone's hand, look them in the eye and ask for the vote, they greatly improve their chances in the election. In radio, when listeners meet you, have a personal exchange with you, no matter how brief, you greatly improve your chances to turn them into one of your fans. They've met you! They feel they *know* you. They'll be proud to tell others that they met a celebrity.

Wherever you go, carry pictures and gift certificates for small prizes with you, and be sure that every member of your show is doing the same. Introduce yourself every chance you get, and humbly ask people to listen to you on the radio. You'll be self-conscious at first, but as you become more comfortable with it, you'll impact a *lot* of potential new listeners in the course of a year.

In politics, the candidate that wins is the one who meets the most people in person during the campaign. In radio, you're constantly campaigning!

-66-

PUBLICITY PICTURES

Top Of
Mind
Awareness:
The
ability of
your
audience
to remem-
ber they
listen to
you. High
awareness
leads to
increased
ratings,
and a
positive
"phantom
cume"
effect.

Does your show have publicity photos? All celebrities have them, and it's even more important for radio personalities to have them because it gives listeners (and potential listeners) a chance to put a face with the name. Unless you're hideously ugly, of course. In that case, use a caricature!

When they meet you, and feel that they know you, they are more likely to listen to you and tell other people about you. They will feel special because of their connection to you.

Publicity photos make great handouts for listeners at your appearances and events, but there are a lot more uses for them as well.

Is your picture on the walls at restaurants where they display the pictures of famous people who eat there? Why not? If you're embarrassed about asking to have the photo hung, get an intern or producer to do it for you.

When you give away a prize on or off the air, be sure an autographed picture is included. No, you don't talk about that on the air. Simply write a note on your picture expressing your thanks for listening. It personalizes the experience for the listener.

McDonald's changed fast-food forever by including a toy in each specially packaged meal sold to children. Their marketing has affected the "decision maker" (mom) by those who are closest to her (little Johnny) by going one step further in reaching out. When the time comes to decide where to take the kids for lunch, those "Happy Meals" often tilt the scale in the favor of the golden arches. Never underestimate the "little things" you can do to create a bond with your audience.

understand that you are NOT unforgettable. Listeners have a short attention span, and if you are out of sight,
eventually you become "out of mind".
And being out of mind is even worse
than not being "top of mind".

-67-

LETTERS POSTED AT BUSINESSES

Here's another great method of getting some free "buzz" or word of mouth. Every time you talk about a business on the air, endorse a product, or give out a "plug", send a picture, along with a letter on station letterhead that strokes the business. They'll love you for it, and you'll probably end up with that letter in a frame on their wall. Businesses love it when a celebrity uses and recommends their products!

Take this a step further by sending an air check with your "plug" of their business! This takes a little more time and effort, but makes a huge impression on these listeners and businesses!

To have a more dramatic impact, deliver the letter in person. Or at the very least, ask an assistant or intern to contact the manager and deliver it.

Whenever you contact any business, you should score points with your sales department by notifying the local sales manager of your activity. They can then follow up the lead, and hopefully turn it into an advertising agreement on your show.

Not only will you elevate your market presence, it may lead to an endorsement deal and put some cash in your pocket. That's not your primary motivation of course, but a lucrative by-product.

From The Desk Of...Brendan Behan

"All publicity is good, except an obituary notice."

-Brendan Behan, Irish playwright

-68-

Public Appearances

B e prepared when you host those charity events, introduce artists or appear at supermarket grand openings! Know the audience, their expectations and prepare to promote something on your station and your show. Don't waste the opportunity by just going out and "winging it".

Most stations make a huge mistake in assuming that their audience knows that you are on a *radio station*. That's a fatal mistake, like a politician assuming that voters know the pros and cons of candidates of an election. You'd be amazed at how many potential listeners have no clue that your clever station name represents a radio station. Keep in mind that you have to help listeners, and future listeners, understand *how* to use your show and your radio station.

Public appearances are important. Listeners are thrilled to meet you. It's a great way to make them feel like they know you. That's a first step to getting them to like you, and making yourself likable is a key ingredient in making them listen. So don't treat your opportunities to meet the public as a nuisance.

Don't hide! Be upfront. Go out of your way to shake hands, look listeners in the eye and introduce yourself.

I've said it before, but it needs to be repeated again: Be prepared (yes, the Boy Scouts have it right)! You won't be successful in raising your profile without a lot of sweat!

Work the room!

Most personalities are willing to make an effort to appear in public when they first start at a new station. As the newness wears off and their insecurity begins to fade, the appearances become fewer and farther between. This is a fatal mistake. As you become well known, it's more important than ever to continue doing the things that helped you become successful. Don't change. Fame should not change you, nor should it change your work ethic.

Now, when you're out at an event, be sure to put your best foot forward. Make sure attention is paid to details. Work with your promotions department and support staff to help you make an impact. Here are a few ways you can do so:

1. Play a tape of your show, or of your station, at the event, especially before and after your appearance. It should be a commercial-free demo of your station. Don't play your station live. You want to demonstrate the very best aspects of what you are all about.

2. Distribute fliers or brochures about yourself, your show, and your station. Use the opportunity to promote yourself and upcoming events or bits.

3. If it's a charitable event, be sure your logo is displayed prominently on all promotional merchandise. Work with the organization to provide better, larger placement.

4. Finally, spend some preparation time to brain-

storm how you can get to the emotional connection available at each event. Figure out what listeners are thinking about, and come up with a plan to make yourself memorable! In case your station doesn't have one, here's a convenient form to use for appearances. Form courtesy lured.com

---

PERSONAL APPEARANCE REQUEST

REQUESTED BY:_____DATE:_____

CLIENT:_____

ADDRESS:_____

DATE OF APPEARANCE:_____

PERSONALITY REQUESTED:_____

APPROVED: _____   _____
                          YES   NO

Thinking things through will increase your promotional effectiveness!

-69-

PRESS RELEASES

Your show has moments worthy of media coverage! How can you take advantage of it to insure that you get the media exposure you deserve? Most stations rely on sending out a press release, and leave it at that. Well, guess what? Most press releases don't work! And most stations waste a lot of time creating ineffective releases that have no impact.

Don't get me wrong. Press releases can be important, if they are used properly.

First, don't overdo it. You know how many PSA's and requests for air time you get via mail, fax, phone and email? The TV stations get more! Your press release is treated with the same care and consideration as the ones you receive. So, the first rule is to *only send out a press release if what you are doing is really newsworthy.* Make sure that what you are doing is something worth covering, from the media's point of view. Otherwise, you desensitize the directors and editors every time they see something coming from you.

When you send one, *make sure it gets to the right person*! If you're trying to attract television coverage, get the release into the right hands! Contact each assignment editor personally. Sending it to the "news director" is a sure way to find the circular file.

When you deliver your press release, *do something to stand out*. Write objectively, and factually, but be creative when you deliver the press release. Just like sending out a resume', you're competing with hundreds of other candidates to stand out and get noticed. That's why you have to have a "hook" .

Many times, you have a better chance to secure coverage if you tie in a charity. In your press release, *emphasize the charity angle*. This will make it easier for TV to accept and hopefully cover your stunt or bit.

Finally, *follow up your press release with a phone call*. You should already have a working relationship with most of your media contacts. Use that relationship by following up with a personal conversation, if only to ask if the press release arrived, and if you can help answer any questions.

Taking it one step further, you might even solicit some friends to call the front desk at TV stations on the day of the event asking "what's happening right now at ____ " Most receptionists will route those calls through to the assignment editor on duty, and could spur some interest in covering your story.

Press releases have value, if used properly. Even a *great* release won't guarantee coverage, but can be instrumental in attracting some attention. Use the example provided on the following page to help guide you in preparing yours.
January 14, 2002

Bob & Dave are Homeless!

Beginning Monday, WXXX morning show hosts Bob & Dave will be homeless. No, they haven't been fired (yet!). The wacky morning duo will be living on the streets of Springfield as if they were homeless.

Hook

The idea was inspired by a call to WXXX's Bob & Dave morning show on Thursday. The caller was a single mother of two young children who had been evicted from her apartment, had nowhere to go and nothing to eat. Her story touched Bob & Dave deeply, and the idea to live as homeless people themselves was created in an effort to relieve the pain and suffering of homeless people in the county.

Why

Warmth/ heart

During their homeless ordeal (Monday-Friday), Bob & Dave will encourage listeners to donate blankets, coats, clothing, food and cash at the WXXX studios, on Radio Lane. Their goal is to raise $50,000 in cash and contributions during their homeless week. The Springfield Homeless Shelter will collect the contributions for distribution.

What it is

Charity

Asked about the event, Bob commented, "Dave and I have always been active in helping the homeless, but when we heard that caller on Thursday morning, it became personal. We realized that there are some

Quote to use in case they don't come out

devastating stories. WXXX is committed to doing whatever we can to help."

For more information, or to arrange interviews, pictures or coverage of Bob & Dave's Homeless Adventure, contact: Dawn in WXXX Promotions, (888) 888-8888.

Contact info

Keep your press releases short and to the point. Remember the KISS principle (Keep It Simple Stupid). The value of the KISS formula is illustrated in the following story:

In 1960 Bennett Cerf bet Theodore Seuss Geisel (aka Dr. Seuss) $50 that he couldn't write an entire book using only fifty words. The result was *Green Eggs and Ham*. What a great example that length of the bit has nothing to do with the entertainment delivered. By the way, Cerf never paid the $50.

PRESS RELEASE WORK SHEET

PRIORITY Number 1-6

_____WHO_____

_____WHAT_____

_____WHERE_____

_____WHEN_____

_____WHY_____

_____HOW_____

Write a PRIMARY ANGLE. (What makes this newsworthy?)

_____

_____

_____

Write a SECONDARY ANGLE. (Another newsworthy reason slanted toward a specific medium of contact.)

_____

_____

What Other information must be included in this release? (Co-sponsors, personality names, companies providing prizes, ticket locations, etc.)

_____

_____

Write a few short, compelling headlines for this release. _____

_____

_____

_____

Press Release worksheet courtesy www.lured.com

-70-

TELEVISION

The first step is *preparing* for television coverage. If your show is easy to work with, you'll be the first phone call from TV stations whenever they need that "B-Roll" for a story they are covering. It's not difficult to prepare your studio to be television-friendly. Have your engineers provide a direct audio feed for camera crews to plug into when they arrive. It simplifies everything for them, and it sounds better.

Make sure your studio is decorated with your station logo in all possible locations. This insures that your call letters will be on display. There's nothing more frustrating than doing a great piece for TV, and not receive credit when the story airs. At the minimum, you should display a large station logo in every camera angle shot. Put small logos on each telephone and the vu meters. For some reason, television stations love to show the meters bouncing while the personality is talking. Don't forget microphone flags as well! You might also keep a station shirt (or a shirt that promotes your show) on hand for each member of the show to slip on if you find that a reporter is stopping by as well.

If you want to take it up a notch, help the camera crew by installing television lighting. You can switch them on whenever needed.

When interviewed on television, be sure to work your call letters and/or the name of your show in frequently. Instead of just responding with a simple answer, work in the call letters. Don't give them sound bites that can be edited to keep the story intact but reduce your credit!

From The Desk Of...Timothy Crouse

"A lightweight, by definition, is a man who cannot assert his authority over the national press, cannot manipulate reporters, cannot finesse questions, prevent leaks or command a professional public relations operation."

-Timothy Crouse, on covering presidential candidates, in the book, *The Boys on the Bus*

See *Morning Radio I,* Chapter 7 for a full discussion on what it takes to be properly prepared

Preparation: Great talent understands that shows sound more spontaneous (not to mention topical and funny) when they are more prepared. You can't go into a show cold and "wing it". Letterman has a team of writers that spend most of the day preparing a Top 10 List so that Dave can sound spontaneously funny each night! There's a major difference between collecting data and properly preparing your material.

PART 6:
MISCELLANEOUS
THOUGHTS ON OTHER
IMPORTANT MATTERS

-71-

CHARITY PROMOTIONS

Why do charity work, or charity promotions? Obviously, the publicity you provide yields a benefit to your community and creates a good feeling for your station.

You're also likely to further a positive image for your show, and perhaps even make contact with community leaders that can help you at some point.

But face it. The biggest reason you spend time on your show talking about nonprofit organizations is to create talk and press for your show. There's nothing wrong with that. Publicity for your show is a good thing, and in the process, the charity's profile is increased with yours.

So, before getting involved in an event, make sure you control the idea. Raising money for research to combat breast cancer is a great charitable cause. If your audience target is adult women, you're right on the money with the topic. But an on-air campaign highlighting the problem isn't nearly as effective as Bras Across (your local landmark). Listeners raise money and awareness for breast cancer by contributing bras, which are strung together for a great visual event, television coverage and tremendous awareness for the charity and your show!

When you commit to a charitable cause, adopt it as your own, and make it personal and meaningful, a secondary benefit emerges. The audience will cut you some slack for other outrageous things you do that they consider in poor taste or "over the line". The next time you mildly offend your listener (and you're not doing your job if you don't create *some* complaints), you'll be easily forgiven because of your generous nature and warm heart.

Many shows who are heavily involved in charities become shy about the press they receive as a result. Don't feel bad about it when listeners give you the credit for your efforts! Even if your true motivation is publicity, it doesn't diminish the charity work. Your willingness to do what it takes to win doesn't make you dishonest, and your efforts will benefit many others. If you work hard in the setup and design of your charitable campaign, you will become more sensitive to what people want, what they respond to. That makes you more successful, and enriches the lives of others. Exploiting that as a strength is not just opportunitstic and good business, it does good for the public.

From The Desk Of...Joseph H. DeFrees

If it's not in the best interest of the public, it's not in the best interest of business

Do your charitable promotions speak to the audience's mind or to their hearts? You will win your audience when you appeal to their emotions. You will never impact an audience by trying to convince them that what you are doing is a good idea. You can be successful if you make it meaningful, personal and touch them deeply. Pour your heart into your charity events.

If you don't get credit with listeners for your charity causes, why bother? The effort should be productive <u>and</u> rewarding. Productive for the "good" it does in the community. Rewarding for the "goodwill" it does for your station!

-72-

ADOPTING A CHARITY

Most radio stations do a great deal of charity work. They are constantly promoting the blood drive, a community race or an event to find the cure for a disease. While their intentions are good, their efforts admirable, and results impressive, most stations fail to generate any lasting recognition for all they do.

In order to make an impact, you should strongly consider the benefits of finding a charity that you are strongly involved with, and "adopt" it as the sole beneficiary of all of your efforts. If you're more industrious, you could even start your own!

In Dallas, Kidd Kraddick founded Kidd's Kids, a charity that helps sick children. In San Diego, Jeff & Jer, with the support of Star 100.7 helped launch a campaign that led to building a transitional shelter for domestic abuse called Becky's House.

As you develop your strategy for selecting a charity to work with, consider these points:

1. **Be specific**. In 1995, following the Oklahoma City bombing, many stations participated in the relief effort. But KSTZ/Des Moines did a teddy bear

drive called "Bears Because Iowa Cares". The bears were shipped directly to Oklahoma City victim relief efforts to help aid in the healing process. The promotion struck a cord with listeners who felt helpless in a desperate situation. The station gave them a chance to participate in something more tangible than simply raising money, and it made it easy for listeners to feel like they were helping.

2. **Be involved with the right cause.** Aligning with a charity can win valuable image credits, but choosing the right charity is the key to a successful venture. You must know your listeners, what they care about and what they will support before choosing a charity to back. Is there a local issue that is more beneficial than a national one?

3. **If you aren't fully committed, don't bother.** You must sound like you really believe in the cause, or it

---

From The Desk Of...Terry Anderson

With all the terrible things that happen, with all the terrible people, I'm still an optimist. I still believe in the goodness of people.

-Terry Anderson is a former US hostage in Lebanon

---

will show. Slight hints of detachment will alienate listeners and plant a negative image in listener minds about your sincerity. As stated in *Morning Radio*, the great shows always sound sincere.

4. **Be persistent.** Keep at it, do the "little" things and never give up. Many shows place a great deal of effort in launching a campaign, but drop it just as it is getting to the point of paying off. Many times, the efforts are wasted because they haven't invested enough time to reap the benefits. Other times, shows become distracted by obstacles in their path and lack the focus, drive and determination to work through difficult situations and reach the goal. Never give up. Never surrender.

   In ancient times, a King had a boulder placed on a roadway. Then he hid himself and watched to see if anyone would remove the huge rock. Some of the King's wealthiest merchants and courtiers came by and simply walked around it. Many loudly blamed the king for not keeping the roads clear, but none did anything about getting the stone out of the way.

   Then a peasant came along carrying a load of vegetables. Upon approaching the boulder, the peasant laid down his burden and tried to move the stone to the side of the road. After much pushing and straining, he finally succeeded. After the peasant picked up his load of vegetables, he noticed a purse lying in the road where the boulder had been. The purse contained many gold coins and a note from the king indicating that the gold was for the person who removed the boulder from the roadway.

The peasant learned what many of us never understand: Every obstacle presents an opportunity to improve our condition.

Success of a morning show will be determined only by your ability to entertain the public in the manner the public most wants to be entertained.

ON PERSISTENCE:

Adam Sandler is not the funniest performer in America, but he is one of the most prepared and his work ethic is unmatched. He spends a part of *every* morning writing new material. His commitment to his craft, drive, persistence and determination has made him one of Hollywood's most successful comics.

Nothing you do will take the place of persistence. The world is full of individuals with talent that fail to succeed because they don't have the intestinal fortitude to persist!

For details on how to understand your audience, and design a show to appeal to them, refer to *Morning Radio 1*, Chapter 5

-73-

Making Sales Demands Work

It's not good. It's not bad. It just *is*. Those value added requests (demands) from your sales department. They're constantly bugging you for more to sell. Sponsorships. Giveaways. Features. You name it, they'll slap an advertiser on it. Stations have so many demands for promotions or features, your station can easily be overwhelmed!

Many of these promotions, especially if they're poorly conceived, only clutter the sound and confuse the listener. How can you cope?

1. Don't let them attach the name of your show or station to your personality oriented features.

2. Be clever with wording. If the prize isn't a great one, don't let your show take credit for the giveaway. If you can, refuse to give away prizes with little or no appeal to your listeners. If you're forced into a weak contest, get rid of it as quickly as possible. And finally, distance your show from the weak contest. Instead of WXXX giving away a jar of mustard, make sure you say the mustard company is giving it away.

3. Refuse contests that qualify listeners for a bigger prize. Insist on simplicity and program to the listener's mindset of "instant gratification".

4. Think it through. Pre-plan. Include all key decision makers on your management team early in the planning process. This will avoid problems as the promotion develops.

-74-

SCREENING YOUR CALLS

If you want to attract great callers on the air, you have to PUT great calls on the air!   There are several great reasons to do so, and believe it or not, caller *content* is not the primary consideration.

The quickest way to project your image is to carefully choose callers that project the image you desire. Callers represent the type of person that listeners will assume make up the majority of your calls. After all, people have a natural tendency to want to be around others that are like them, share similar tastes and lifestyles. You may be targeting a specific demographic or psychographic, but if most of your callers are dissimilar to those goals, you're sending a message that this show is for someone else.

I once managed a very talented morning show that took great pride in taking stupid callers and turning them into rib-splitting entertainment. He was *very* good at it, but I am convinced that it made an unspoken statement about the type of listener that the show attracted, and ultimately prevented him from greater success.

Another consideration in screening calls is to realize that callers are *not* typical listeners. In many cases they are not even *real people*. They are a completely, totally different animal from a listener. As Premiere Radio's talk host Phil Hendrie puts it, "A caller is someone who has bumper stickers on their car. They write letters to their Senator, TV or radio stations. They fancy themselves to be activists. They may mumble to themselves on a park bench somewhere. They are strange people."

Just because someone calls to be on the air does not entitle them ,or qualify them, to be on with you. You must evaluate whether or not the caller will improve your show! It is hard to screen calls. You often find yourself in a position of being rude to people.

Callers are merely props for talent. They are to be used to make the show more interesting. If the caller isn't entertaining, the prop isn't working!

Details on how to screen calls and what to look for in callers: See *Morning Radio 1: Chapter 14*

-75-

TELLING STORIES

Everyone has heard radio referred to as "Theater of the Mind". Never underestimate what an incredibly powerful tool the spoken word is in reaching listeners. According to an article in *Forbes* magazine, famed entertainer Peter Ustinov was performing a one-man show in New Zealand when the power went out. In the dark, Ustinov changed his approach with the following announcement, "The performance goes on. From now on, I'm on the radio. You're having a sleepless night and you switch the bedside radio on. Ready? Here goes…". For the next 20 minutes, Ustinov performed in pitch black, using vocal inflection to compensate for the lack of visual contact. Following the performance, he evaluated the audience response, "I got more laughs than when they couldn't see me. When the lights went on again, it wasn't at all the same. I regretted that the lights never went off again."

Since the beginning of time, humans have been telling

From The Desk Of…Carl W. Buechner

They may forget what you said, but they will never forget how you made them feel

---

stories. Parents read or tell stories to newborns. Your listeners love stories. Air personalities who are able to create a story and effectively relate it to the audience make a lot of money.

There is a story behind all of your personality traits. The stories include what you drive, where you live, owner or renter, what kind of pets you have, what your hobbies are, and more. Your story is defined by your attitudes, opinions, lifestyle, choices, values and morals. Every time information is related to your audience, whether it's a daily life experience or information, it offers an opportunity to craft the story. Don't just present facts or data. Make it meaningful by sharing your experiences in story form, whether it's 30 seconds or 30 minutes. Dig deeply to find those stories and your listeners will feel like they know something about you.

It's your challenge to find those stories and embellish them on the air. There's nothing wrong with a little fiction in your show. This is show biz, and you are the actor or actress that makes the material come alive. One of the stations I worked with had just hired an aspiring young actress to be part of their developing morning show. Though her knowledge of radio consisted almost exclusively of how to turn one on and off, she had an intense passion for learning the art of morning radio and becoming successful.

In a session with the program director and all of the members of the show, the issue of role identification was raised. The show consisted of the main "DJ", a straight news and traffic person, and a sidekick who was new to radio from acting. The main morning DJ, a veteran of morning radio, and obviously well-read in the contemporary application of morning radio culture, declared, "I have to be who I am on the air to be believable. I want to be *real*." After convincing him that his life and his personality just wasn't all that exciting, the actress summarized it beautifully. "Hey, just tell me what you want me to be, what is going to make this show successful, and I will play that role. I don't know anything about radio, but the role of an actress is to accept the role and find herself in it, to pour out emotion in that role and make herself vulnerable in the character so the audience can identify with her and feel a strong connection to her." Perfect. Couldn't have said it better myself.

Or, as Bubba The Love Sponge puts it, "…it's show biz. Rocky's not the heavy weight champion of the world. Bruce Willis isn't *Die Hard* when he goes home."

So, creative story telling is about embellishing material into content. It usually begins with actual experiences, but other times it is completely fabricated. However, if the fiction you create on the air is based on reality, it will be much easier for your character to perform.

Syndicated talk show host Phil Hendrie is one of the best practitioners of combining radio and theater. His talk show combines live improvisation, theater and interactive dialogue with the listener playing a "role" in his play. Hendrie describes his show, "Is it a bit or is it theater? I present characters on a stage not unlike what they do in the movies or on TV for the entertainment of my audience. To say it is a bit is incorrect. It is theater." With his cast of 20-plus characters (he performs all of them), Hendrie is able to perform controversial material that many hosts would not be able to get away with. Hendrie is a perfect example of a personality that effectively combines incredible story-telling abilities with a sense of dramatic flair. Simultaneously, his personality and point of view brilliantly shine through the characters.

The best material for your show is probably based on your personal life. If you avoid talking about your personal life on the radio, you're missing one of the most endearing tools you could employ in your arsenal. But knowing how to tell those stories, how to relate those stories to the audience, and how to embellish those stories is what separates the "inside" shows from the relatable ones.

How can you increase your chances of being likeable? Use positive words. Use positive words and phrases, not negative ones. Ask a kid who has just been to Disneyland about their experience, and they'll tell you how great it was. Ask an adult who accompanied the child, and they'll tell you that the lines were long, it was too hot and parking was horrendous, but it "wasn't bad". Children tell you what it IS. Adults tell you what it ISN'T. Who is more FUN to be around? Adults or kids? Which is more positive? Avoid the vocabulary of DON'T.

-76-

How To Tell Stories

The mechanics of successful story telling on the air follow the same pattern as with any bit or promotion. Of course, the story is only compelling to an audience if the audience first feels a connection to the storyteller. It is essential that you make them *like* you. Being likeable doesn't necessarily mean being liked as a person, but you must make the audience warm to your personality. Then, you are ready to 'hook' the audience. Like a great ad campaign, you have a short window of opportunity to attract interest in your story. Most personalities have great ideas, and most have terrific material. But the ones who can find the words to hook the audience have the key to unlock the imagination.

Next, you must convince the audience to play along with you, engaging them in the tale, and accepting your character. You do this with details (set up) and embellishment (dress up). The audience will be able to "see" the story through your eyes, and enter your world through *your* point of view. This is where you have a chance to shine, to showcase your art. Imagine you are telling the story to a child. Go into great detail with specific descriptions to paint an exciting picture so the bit comes alive for them. As Rudyard Kipling put it, "Words are, of course, the most powerful drug used by mankind." Your words can have a powerful effect on your listeners. Choose them carefully, prepare them properly and deliver them with passion.

When you're able to get them to this point, you have them. If your concentration slips for a moment, you loosen your hold over their attention. Be fearless, and move on into the punch line (payoff).

Finally, know when (and how) the story *ends* before you ever begin to tell it. Just as a comedian will write the punchline before he or she constructs the set-up, you should know how your story will "pay off". This allows you to visualize your performance. Combined with mental discipline to remain focused on your performance, knowing how the story ends will create confidence, energy and direction. You'll be able to leave the audience with a good feeling (or at least a desired, predictable feeling that you control), as if you were writing the final scene of a play! Then, when you bring down the curtain (blackout), you'll receive their approval, and you can move on! The last image you leave will be their lasting impression of your bit, your show, and of *you*.

When preparing your bits, or stories, know the end of the story before you begin to tell it. Telling stories usually leads to listener involvement, and it always leads to better character definition. If you set up a theme or topic with your own story, it "primes the pump" for listener feedback and interaction, and you'll get a much more emotional listener on your phones if they feel like you are their friend.

Just as an accomplished golfer visualizes his shot before addressing the ball, you should have a mental image of how your material is going to sound before you begin.

CREATING STORY LINES WITH A "DRAMATIC ARC"

Originally titled "Why Your Morning Show Sucks"
By Mark Ramsey, Nova Marketing Group Inc
The original article appeared in Radio Ink magazine

Much has been written and said lately regarding Howard Stern's marital split and his ensuing search for a girlfriend. This sad state of affairs has been credited with spiking Howard's ratings to record levels. But if you fail to read between the lines, you may miss a much more profound truth that is as applicable to your station's morning show as it is to Howard Stern's.

Howard's ordeal, you see, is what a writer would call a "dramatic arc". It's a journey, a story with a beginning, a middle and an end. In the beginning, Howard announced his separation. Now, in the middle, the sex search is on. In the end, Howard will wind up on a date and-knowing him as any listener does-in a relationship. Beginning, middle, end. It is a story covering many months.

Why don't X-Files favorites Mulder and Scully hop into bed? Because that would end their arc; it would finish the story. The "dramatic tension" between the characters would evaporate, and so would the audience. Recently, Mulder finally found his missing sister, effectively ending one mini-arc. When your arc ends (or it's welcome wears out), you need a new one.

These ancient rules of drama apply every bit as much to your morning show, too. The problem with the average morning shows is that they're about "moments", not "stories." Moments are fine. Many stations create moments with stunts during ratings periods (e.g., The X-File's "Cops" episode), but their impact is ephemeral-here today, gone tomorrow. Similarly, we in radio have the obsessive drive to be "topical"-it's all about what's hot NOW. There's no past, no future, just now. In other words, there's no story, no arc to draw the audience and emotionally involve them until that arc ends. There's no direction, no momentum, no exploration of new territory. One day blends into the next.

That's what makes it stale.

I think It's fair to say "staleness" is the single greatest problem facing even the most popular and enduring morning show. The story is old; it has stalled. Now what? "Stale" is not something at which to throw new benchmarks. It's something for which you open a new chapter.

What's so fresh about TV's *Friends* over the past year or so? Why, Chandler and Monica's relationship, of course. It's a new story-a new arc-and it carries the show in a new, fresh direction when previous stories and arcs had ended.

Letterman was in a stale rut until his unfortunate heart

condition effectively ended one arc in time for his return to the show to kickoff another. Is there any question Letterman will be forever different now? You're going to tune in to find out, aren't you?

What are your arcs?

Where are your stories?

Is each day simply a new and self-contained "episode" or is it another developing chapter in a series? Do listeners recall only bits, or do they remember "stories"? Do listeners eagerly anticipate a new chapter tomorrow morning, or have they been trained to expect more of the same, day in and day out: "Battle of the Sexes" at 7:20, "Name It and Win" at 8:15, etc? The purpose of benchmarks is to cue listeners to the times they're listening to your station and give them a chance to play along; their purpose should not be to serve as a substitute for a story.

A morning show should be like a soap opera-a continuing story, unfolding one chapter at a time. This is what creates history for the characters. It's why Stern's fans know so much about him that trivia books have been published on the topic. It's what transforms a personality from somebody funny you laugh with to somebody real you care about.

Many of your stations are obsessed about hiring new producers and writers to fix what is broken. But the answer is beyond choreographing musical microphones and scripting fresh gags. The answer is to create a story! When we demand so little of the audience, it's no wonder we get so little in return.

You can improve your ability to tell great stories. Work on it! Learn to tell the same story five different ways, each time keeping interesting and entertaining. Practice the art of story-telling with your children, your family, your co-workers. Better yet, work on telling the same story to the same person three different times and see if you can make it entertaining and fresh each time they hear it!

From The Desk Of...Jackie Torrence

Radio put technology into storytelling and made it sick. TV killed it. Then you were locked into somebody else's sighting of that story. You no longer had the benefit of making that picture for yourself, using your imagination.

-Jackie Torrence *African American storyteller*

-78-

CAPTURING THE MOMENT/ DEALING WITH TRAGEDY

One of the most important things you can do as a a morning show is find a way to become *the* show to tune in when something major happens. Weather emergencies, local tragedies and city-wide celebrations create opportunities for your show to increase your value to your audience.

The ability to "capture the moment" can be the difference between success and failure. If you are able to identify those moments when they occur, react quickly and tap into your audience's reaction with an emotional sincerity, you can make giant strides in your goal of attaining local celebrity status.

Whether it's a natural event (a disaster), or an event you create, your ability to turn a topic into an experience for your audience can raise your profile to the next level.

One of the most difficult shows you will ever perform is the day of, or day after, a tragedy strikes your community. I've heard dozens (hundreds?) of shows simply "give up" and avoid addressing the very topic that literally *everyone* in town is talking about. While it's true that most shows are not equipped to cover major events as well as television and news radio, shows that don't deal with these emergencies are not only letting their listeners down, they're missing an opportunity.

In the 80s, following a major earthquake in Los Angeles, KIIS-FM's Rick Dees abandoned his normal morning show format to let listeners talk. He provided a forum for Los Angeles residents to share their emotions, their feelings, their thoughts and concerns.

When a high school shooting occurred in San Diego, STAR 100.7 morning superstars Jeff & Jer stayed on the air until 1pm taking calls and passing on information. Through the confusion of trying to sort out a major breaking news story, Jeff & Jer took calls from parents of the students at the school who had not heard from their children. At the school, their producer "Little" Tommy Sablan then found the kids for a tearful, powerful emotional reunion on the air.

Great shows, and shows that become great, are so in touch with the lives of their listener, it's almost a natural response to do "the right thing" in difficult times and connect with an audience. You don't have to be an authority on the topic to deal with it. You just have to be alert enough to understand your audience well enough to connect.

What does your show do when an event occurs that affects your listener's lives? A few weeks after Princess Diana's death, I had the opportunity to participate in Don Anthony's Morning Show Boot Camp. It was amazing how many shows admitted they did *nothing* on the air the morning after her death. Excuses ranged from "It's too depressing" to "That's not what we do" to "That's all TV was talking about and we wanted to be different". I was amazed, somewhat appalled and became concerned about the future of personality radio. When radio stations fail to respond to events that impact our listener's world, we make our radio stations irrelevant.

It doesn't have to be anything more than putting average listeners on the air to provide a common experience for your audience to relate. An outlet to express their emotions.
The most important part of preparing yourself for your show is to understand your audience well enough to know how they will react to events. When you are able to "feel" that reaction, you will be able to anticipate events and relate to them in an appropriate way.

Winning morning shows make it a habit of seizing the moment. When events occur that affect their community, they instinctively visualize what they can do on the air to create the moment.

 Don't let skeptics throw you off track. If you listen too much to critics, you'll lose your nerve. Your confidence will falter, and you'll talk yourself out of taking risks. Any time you try something new, different, or out-of-the-box, you will attract criticism from co-workers, friends, the sales department, maybe even your PD. Most broadcasters don't have a vision. They don't see it. To them, they'll "believe it when they see it". They have to have tangible evidence. Listen to them and it'll suck the life and emotion out of your idea. But if you understand your audience, are willing to take risks and f you believe it, you will see it. And if you see it *and* believe it, you will make it happen. It's not easy. It's hard. You must make yourself vulnerable and take a walk in unfamiliar surroundings.

The rewards are great for those who take the risk and execute with passion and precision.

Plan for success. Believe in success. Visualize success. Brainstorm. Plan.

When events or tragedies occur that impact the lives of your listener, ask yourself, "What can our show do to be very good, when things are very bad?"

If you want listeners to talk about you, talk about THEM, and things they CARE about. It's up to you to instinctively feel what is top of mind with your audience, and turn those topics into entertainment.

Experiences don't have to derive from disasters to make memorable radio. Is your show the station listeners use to celebratae community pride? To express anger or concern? To be their outlet? Do they depend on you to represent them and enable them to feel a part of something?

-79-

LEVERAGING EMOTIONS

Throughout this book, and in *Morning Radio 1*, the importance of appealing to listeners on an emotional level has been emphasized.

In an interview with FMQB magazine (1/5/01), Michelle Stevens (Nassau Broadcasting's Sr. VP/Programming) reviewed the "10 Laws of Leveraging Emotional Connections as follows:**The Law of Lifestyle Psychology.** Being in touch with the psychology of your audience. Talk about the things your listeners are talking about. But first, you must understand the attitudes, culture and events that shaped the mindset of your target audience. Identify real emotions, use thought starters.

The Law of Bonding. Speak in your listener's vocabulary, drop the "jock spiel" and speak one on one to your "friend" (a.k.a.-listener). Think about the different way you speak to an acquaintance versus a close friend. Speak to your listener as your companion, share with them, kid with them, confide and relate like you are their best friend, rather than some disembodied voice talking at them. Be careful not to force emotion as it could backfire into a fake or condescending approach.

The Law of Relating-"The Oprah Phenomenon".

She is one of the wealthiest women in America, yet relates to the average, everyday woman…and the average woman relates and connects with her. She talks about the things that are important to the common everyday woman. She shows her vulnerable side and talks about her weight issues, childhood, etc. The real stars don't act like stars-they act like the common person, sharing the same feelings and experiences and that's what makes them stars.

The Law of Shared Experience.

It's the little things that truly have the biggest impact. Incorporate real life relatable material into content. Think Seinfeld. Everyday, real life situations and observations let the audience into your daily life…embarrassing moments, silly problems, and everyday situations. Your listeners/friends want to know that you have kids, go to the supermarket, and do the same things that they do. This can be as simple as weaving a relatable into a generic weather forecast: "You may be wearing a tank top and shorts picking the Christmas tree this weekend…sunny and 75.' The bonding power of this type of referencing in content and station imaging keeps us "high touch" as real companions, experiencing and finding humor in real life situations.

The Law of Balance.

React emotionally to both humorous situations and difficult tragedies. Cover the spectrum of emotions: humor, tragedy, social awareness, addressing the topical and social issues that are important to your target lifegroup and community. Become a relatable, responsive personality.

The Law of Storytelling. The greatest speakers, authors, screenwriters, songwriters and politicians of all time have harnessed the power of storytelling to form bonds and strike an emotional chord within us.

The Law of Simplicity. Avoid pitfalls that inhibit emotional bonding: Talking at or down to listeners, production that muddies the message and sounds good to radio guys, but not the real listener; inside jokes, slick clichés and meaningless inside radio words.

The Law of Presentation. Execute with your heart and soul. There is no replacement for passion.

The Law of Discipline. The Theory of Loose and Tight. All things in life combine loose and tight. Utilize strong break structure, yet sound relaxed. This is planned spontaneity. Have the discipline to keep your break focused and simple. Too many great breaks turn into poor breaks because they go on too long. Leave them wanting more and they'll keep coming back. A great example is the hit TV show *Survivor.* It aired *once* a week. America couldn't wait until Wednesday, and people planned their week around being available at 8pm.

From The Desk Of...New York Times

Radio lets people see things with their own ears.

-From an editorial in January, 1986

-80-

What's Your Character?

In *Morning Radio 1*, a great deal of attention is devoted to developing your on-air character. Here is a checklist that can point you in the right direction:

1. What do you *stand* for?
2. Are you genuine and believable?
3. Are you seen as sharing and caring for your listeners?
4. Are you willing to *get involved?*
5. Do you know what and who makes your community "work"?
6. Do you work hard to stay visible in the community?
7. Does your lifestyle reflect, or appeal to, your target audience?
8. Are you *original?*
9. Do you have a sense of humor? What is that sense of humor?
10. Are you willing to be vulnerable, and let your emotions show through?

-81-

How to Measure Success

If you're like 90% of the air personalities and programmers in the world, the single most important means of measuring your value is the quarterly ratings. It's the equivalent of a report card. If you are to fulfill your ultimate potential, not to mention preserve your sanity, this must change.

Rather than placing so much emphasis on the upcoming trend or quarterly report, take it upon yourself to focus on deriving your satisfaction from the process of creating dynamic, memorable radio. In doing so, you will come to appreciate the details, the preparation, the execution and the process of your art form. Day in, day out. Week in, week out. Year in, year out.

Failure is not achieving your potential. If you come in each morning fully prepared, focus on creating entertainment that matters to your audience and execute your plan to the very best of your ability, you will never *lose*. The ratings gods may not always smile on you, but you will not be a failure.

In the big picture, a single ratings period is meaningless. Strive for consistent excellence in the process of creating emotional moments on the air. There are many inaccuracies in the ratings system, and audience results will never fully measure reality. If you keep your eye on the things that matter most, and let the ratings take care of themselves. The reward of ratings success will come when you strive for excellence rather than reward.

.

From The Desk Of...Ralph Waldo Emerson

"So much of our time is preparation, so much is routine, and so much retrospect, that the pith of each man's genius contracts itself to a very few hours."

-From "Experience", 1844

-82-

JOHN WOODEN

Former UCLA basketball coach John Wooden is recognized as one of the greatest basketball coaches in history. His 10 NCAA Championships is unmatched, and no coach has gained the honor and respect of Coach Wooden. In his book, *Wooden: A Lifetime of Observations and Reflections On and Off The Court,* he lists the most important things for success. The suggestions can be applied to your show, and your life!

1. Fear no opponent. Respect every opponent.

2. It's perfection of the smallest details that make big things happen.

3. Hustle makes up for many a mistake.

4. Be more interested in character than reputation.

5. Be quick, but don't hurry.

6. The harder you work, the more luck you will have.

7. Know that valid self-analysis is crucial for improvement.

8. Failing to prepare is preparing to fail.

PART 7: HOLIDAYS

A COMPREHENSIVE PROMOTION

GUIDE

Holidays present a particular challenge for many shows. How do you stand out from the crowd and relate to your audience when their attention is more likely than ever to be on the leisure activities they have planned?

A lot of stations take an unusual, or bizarre, approach to gaining attention. Doing the unexpected-like giving away a vascectomy a day for Valentines' week-has become more popular in the last few years. If you are planning a promotion like this, be sure to study the section on stunts.

When a holiday approaches, be creative and plan ahead. Remember that the most important goal is to reflect the mood of your audience, and relate to their lifestyle.

This section is a good place to start, but it's just that-a start! It contains a fairly detailed reference guide for all of the major (and some not so major) holidays, along with ideas to help you make it come alive on the air. But like any idea, your success will depend on your ability to craft these ideas into your show, your personality and your on-air character!

-83-

HAPPY NEW YEAR!

Celebrating the end of one year and the start of a new one is an age-old religious, social, and cultural observance in all parts of the world. In Western nations the New Year festivities take place on December 31, but in other cultures (China, for example) the celebrations take place on different dates.

The Jewish New Year, called Rosh Hashana, is sometimes called the "feast of the trumpets." It starts on the first day of the month of Tishri, which may begin any time from September 6 to October 5. The celebration lasts for 48 hours but ushers in a ten-day period of penitence.

The Chinese New Year is celebrated wherever there are sizable Chinese communities. The official celebration lasts one month and begins in late January or early February. There are outdoor parades and fireworks to mark the occasion.

In Japan the New Year festivities take place on January 1 to 3. In some rural areas the time of celebration corresponds more closely to the Chinese New Year, and the dates vary between January 20 and February 19. The house entrance is hung with a rope made of rice straw to keep out evil spirits. Decorations of ferns, bitter orange, and lobster promise good fortune, prosperity, and long life.

The American celebration of the New Year marks the end
of the Christmas holiday period. Many people go to church
on New Year's Eve, and many attend parties. Street
celebrations in large cities are televised. New Year's Day
itself is often a time for receiving guests at home. And, of
course, what would New Year's Eve be without Dick Clark
dropping the ball in Times Square!

IDEAS TO START THE BRAINSTORMING PROCESS

Instead of a countdown of the past year's songs, feature the
new songs coming out.

Feature **overlooked songs** from the past year, or #1 songs
from the past 20 years.

Produce promos that capture the last 12 months audio, and
set the stage for introducing a "new" or an even **bigger and
better station** or show in the following year.. Mention major
station events and promotions, concerts, local events, etc. Make
it tongue in cheek and humorous (never take yourself too
seriously).

If you do replay the best bits of the year from your morning
show, make it a "**listener requested**" feature (stay humble).
Prime the pump to get it started, and have listeners demand that
you play those classic moments again. Great way to showcase a
new show, and it makes your last few days of the year easier to
prepare!

-84-

New Year's Week Programming

New Year's Eve and New Year's Day wrap up the week that may be the most difficult days of the year to program, promote and reflect in a meaningful way to your audience. If you've ever worked an air shift between Christmas and New Year's, you know that the audience is simply not the same as any other time. The few listeners who are not on vacation are mentally checked out. Add to that the hectic pace in the days leading up to the "big night out" and you get the picture of how difficult it is.

More and more, morning shows take the entire week off, and air a series of "Best Of" features from the previous year.

If you are working in this week, re-negotiate your contract! Seriously, the last week of the year is a good time to invite a **psychic** on the air to predict the events of the coming year. Psychics will always light up the phones and get the show moving, even on the "dead" weeks. Be sure to keep a list of the predictions and check in with them in the last few days of the following year to see if they came true. You can also give away psychic readings.

It's also the right time to run a "**THANKS FOR A GREAT YEAR**" promo...or a "GLAD THE YEAR IS OVER...NEXT YEAR WILL BE EVEN BETTER" campaign from your show. You can make it a warm and friendly promo that lists all the good (and bad) things about the previous year, or make it wacky and funny, depending on your personality. Use a generous amount of local things for topicality and localization. You can even ask listeners to call in their personal items on the morning show, and turn some of those into promos as well.

On Star 100.7/San Diego, Jeff & Jer highlight the first caller of the year and tell listeners to remember that person's name. Then, on their last show of the year, they offer $100 to someone who remembers that first caller's name. Simple, but it's effective.

Some morning shows like to compile a **Time Capsule** each year. They have listeners donate or suggest items to go in from the past year, and predict what will be the most popular trends in the next year. During the last week, you can open last year's time capsule. It's another great way to get the phone to ring in an otherwise dead time.

Whatever you do, it's obvious that if you want to stand out, you have to be even more creative in your approach to year-end programming and promotion. Count on the phones being silent, and plan accordingly. You'll avoid psychiatric bills from the depression of loneliness when the audience

seems like they just aren't out there.

-85-

DRINKING AND DRIVING

An easy and inexpensive way to relate to your audience and score some community service points for New Year's Eve is a week-long "Don't Drink and Drive" or "Designated Driver" campaign on the air. You can start it earlier, and make it work as a month-long campaign that covers Christmas parties too. Work with taxi cabs and limousine companies to provide rides for people too drunk to drive. Use your personalities and celebrities to deliver the messages. You don't have to "finger-wag" to be effective. Here are some copy ideas:

- If someone you know has had too much to drink, take their car keys and throw them up on the house top! Don't drink and Drive....WXXX

- If someone you love has had too much to drink, get them under the mistletoe. While you're giving them a big kiss, reach into their pocket and steal their car keys! Don't drink and drive...WXXX

- Have all the eggnog you want, but if you're drinking, let someone else drive the sleigh. Don't drink and drive...WXXX

- Don't be haunted by the ghost of Christmas parties

past. Designate a driver before you leave for the party. Don't drink and drive...WXXX

- You can be naughty or you can be nice, but not even Scrooge was mean enough to drink and drive. Don't drink and drive...WXXX

- Hey, be safe out there on New Year's Eve…because we need you back next year. Don't drink and drive…WXXX.

On the flip side, if you have a morning show character that is irresponsible, outrageous and over-the-edge, you might be able to get away with some of these on your show. Just be careful you don't run counter to your audience's sensitivity to responsible drinking.

➤ _____ carries a picture of a 6 pack in his wallet.
➤ The zipper was invented in 1642. Had to. Beer was invented the year before.
➤ Some see a half glass of water and say it's half full. Others see it and say it's half empty. _____ sees it and adds a shot of scotch.
➤ He's taking a calcium supplement. His doctor wants his bones to be as hard as his liver.
➤ When _____ was a kid his main ambition was to reach drinking age.
➤ You've had too much if you can use your breath to slash tires.

Know your audience. Know your market, and proceed appropriately. Obviously you won't use this bit on a station that is airing a "responsible drinking" campaign. Know and observe the limits for your market.

-86-

NEW YEAR'S EVE PARTY PATROL

B e everywhere on New Year's Eve! There are so many parties going on that it is difficult to pick the best one to be involved with. So, one approach that works is to pick them ALL and go EVERYWHERE.

Have your station personnel hitting all of the hottest spots in town. Be sure to get "mike" time at each club, at least to be introduced and do your live call-in on the air.

You should, of course, take prizes and party favors with you everywhere you go. Be sure they have your morning show and/or station logo on them prominently.

You could even set up a conference call for all the jocks to be on the air together from different venues for the countdown to the new year.

A variation is to bring the New Years Eve party to your listeners who have no plans for the night. Load up station vehicles and make the rounds to homes with instant parties. You bring the champagne, pizza, videos, music, etc. Do frequent call-ins from the parties you visit. Be sure to drop off official (morning show) Hangover Survival Packages consisting of aspirins, ice packs, earplugs and Bloody Mary Mix, too!

If you're going to do a New Year's Eve party, be prepared to do it BIG, or don't even bother. You're competing with dozens of hotels and venues for customers that night.

Dom Perignon New Year's Celebration Cost Index
(this is a few years old…you'll want to update it to be current):

10. Private reading by Vanity Fair astrologer Michael Lutin, $200.
9. Armani tux, $2100.
8. Breakfast in bed, $35.
7. Presidential Suite at the Plaza Hotel, $15,000.
6. Make-up at Elizabeth Arden, $35.
5. Bottle of Dom Perignon, $90.
4. 10-minute fireworks display, $25,000.
3. Late-night supper at "Sign of the Dove," $175.
2. 2 tickets to "The Nutcracker," $140.
1. Chauffeur-driven Rolls Royce, $1200.

-87-

STAFF NEW YEAR'S EVE PARTY

This is a winner on the air. In mid-December, pick a night and bring in the entire air staff, or just your morning show, to record your New Year's Eve Party in *real time*. Your listeners are invited to eavesdrop on your fun! Cater the evening with great food and drinks and decorate the studio with party favors to set the tone.

Your staff picks all the music and everyone participates in the evening all the way through the playing of Auld Lang Syne and the post-party cleanup for an hour afterwards. It sounds *great* on the air, and reflects the activities that your listeners are experiencing. Be sure to start the playback exactly on time because nothing sounds worse than hitting Auld Lang Syne a few minutes too late!

If you want to take this idea one step further, record another show the next day with the staff counting down the previous year's top songs. In this show, they're tired, hung over, and grumbling about having to clean up, etc.

It can sound great on the air, it's fun to do, and it's a great team-builder!

-88-

NEW YEAR'S EVE CONTESTING

It is always great to have a correspondent from the biggest and best concerts and parties in the country. You could send listeners to the **MTV New Year's Eve Bash** (work with MTV through their marketing and promotions dept. at 212 258-8593) or to New York for New Year's Eve at Times Square. Be sure to arrange for them to call in and be on the air with you!

Another great prize (though expensive) is a **TIME ZONE party.** Your listener wins a cross-country trip for New Year's Eve and goes through all the time zones, celebrating the new year in each place. End the trip in LA, culminating with a visit to the Rose Parade on New Year's Day.

If you can't afford to *send* someone to all the time zones, set up a **network of stations** or parties across the world to bring in the new year. Start with the first person on earth to enter the year (somewhere in the South Pacific), and keep checking in with each time zone until it hits your market.

-89-

NEW YEAR'S RESOLUTIONS

Nearly everyone makes New Year's Resolutions to some extent. Most of us fail to keep them past the Super Bowl, but you can have fun with listeners in the first week of the year. Find an expert that can help your listeners make effective resolutions. Check with local psychiatrists or the sociology department at a local college for their input. You might find someone that makes a great guest.

Another angle is to take calls from listeners on what the New Years Resolution *should* be for celebrities. Have some examples of your own to get it started, but this feature could take over an entire show! A part of this day should be to invite listeners to call and set up resolutions for your show, or members of your show. Be sure you have a thick skin, because if you ask, they'll tell you! It is a great way to make the show sound humble, grounded, down to earth and relatable.

Listeners love to get involved with resolutions they would *like* to make, and think that they really *could* keep! Here's a great list to get you started:

1. Gain weight. At least 30 pounds.
2. Stop exercising. Waste of time.

3. Read less. Makes you think.
4. Watch more TV. I've been missing some good stuff.
5. Procrastinate more. Starting tomorrow.
6. Not date any of the Baywatch cast.
7. Spend more time at work, surfing the internet.
8. Take a vacation to someplace important: like, to see the largest ball of twine.
9. Not jump off a cliff just because everyone else did.
10. Stop bringing lunch from home: I should eat out more.
11. Not have eight children at once.
12. Get in a whole NEW rut!
13. Start being superstitious.
14. Personal goal: bring back disco.
15. Not wrestle with Jesse Ventura.
16. Buy an '83 Eldorado and invest in a really loud stereo system. Get the windows tinted. Buy some fur for the dash.
17. Only wear jeans that are 2 sizes too small and use a chain or rope for a belt. Only wear white T-shirts with those fashionable yellow stains under the arms.
18. Spend my summer vacation in Cyberspace.
19. Not eat cloned meat.
20. Create loose ends.
21. Get more toys.
22. Get further in debt.
23. Break at least one traffic law.
24. Not drive a motorized vehicle across thin ice.
25. Avoid transmission of inter-species diseases.
26. Avoid airplanes that spontaneously drop 1000 feet.
27. Stay off the MIR space station.
28. Not swim with pirhanas or sharks.
29. Associate with even worse business clients.
30. Spread out priorities beyond my ability to keep track of

them.

31. Not take spaceship rides behind comets.
32. Not try to escape from a maximum security prison.
33. Wait around for opportunity.
34. Focus on the faults of others.
35. Mope about my faults.
36. Never make New Year's resolutions again.

For your first show back on in the new year, offer incentives to listeners who are willing to break their resolution live on the air that morning!

This is the perfect time to begin a major, year long promotion. Many stations have capitalized on the promotion, "Greatest Year of your Life". This is a major promotion with many aspects.

-90-

SUPER BOWL

The Super Bowl is not so much a football game as an event. That's why, even if you target women, it is worth the effort to include the Super Bowl in your on-air and promotion plans. In fact, in much the same way that the fashion of the stars overshadows the Grammy Awards, the activities, events and even the *TV commercials* in the Super Bowl create more "buzz" than the game itself.

To help you plans, you should understand how listeners view the big game. For example, did you know that 75% of all viewers indicate that they watch the game in a private home with a gathering of 4-6 people. Many of your listeners make the Super Bowl an annual party that grows each year. In a survey of Americans, when asked, "if given the opportunity to watch the Super Bowl with *anyone they choose*, who would it be?", 53% said their family would come first.

When planning your Super Bowl events, be creative and don't get locked into the trap of simply giving away a big screen TV and pizza. You might want to re-think that party at a nightclub to watch the game, too. In this section, you'll find a summary of various promotion and morning show ideas.

Throw a **Super Bowl House Party**. The whole premise is, "We send you to the Super Bowl, and while you're gone, we get to use your house for our Super Bowl Party." People call in to register themselves for the trip, and tell you about their house. You send interns out to find the best place for your Super Bowl Party with a few select winners. Set up a live broadcast from the house on Super Sunday, and be sure to leave a cash gift behind ($1,000) to cover the damages that will definitely occur. Oh, and be sure your insurance is up to date.

In the **Super Bowl Payoff Weekend**, listeners qualify to win prizes (catered party, free pizza delivery, etc.) whenever they hear a montage of football sounds on your show. It could happen at any moment during the week leading up to the game. That includes during commercials, traffic or newscasts. It's not essential, but a grand prize might be a party in someone's home complete with souvenirs for each team that is playing. Their guests can watch the game from either side, or set up a "cheering room" for each team, complete with cheerleaders (local high schools or colleges will most likely help you out). Take the party over the top by showing up with a big screen TV and surprise the winner by leaving it at their home.

If your audience is more male than female, the **First and 10 Weekend** may make sense. This is a pretty easy mini-promotion for any daypart. Just register the 1st and 10th callers at specific times to win a small prize package. Your callers guess the winner and final score of the game, and whoever comes closest gets a bigger prize on Monday after the game.

More Super Bowl ideas and morning show content at tjohnsonmedia.com

Another popular feature for rock stations that have a heavy composition of males in their audience and maintain music integrity is **Super Bowl Flashback Weekend.** Have the morning show produce intros and then once or twice per hour, play a song that was a big hit in the year of Super Bowl ___. Add a feature to the bit by having the first person with the score of the Super Bowl game that year win a small prize. You could include clips or highlights of Super Bowl games in the produced intros for added effect, if appropriate for your station image.

It doesn't have to be confined to Super Bowl week, but the **Couch Potato** promotion is a winner! Your morning show solicits listeners to submit entries to find the ultimate couch potato in your market. Qualifying listeners must sit on a sofa in the storefront of a high profile furniture store watching TV (your sales department will love this!). They are not allowed to get up for any reason...and no sleeping. Whoever stays there the longest gets a big screen TV, the sofa and a Couch Potato Super Bowl party for his friends. It's up to you whether you want to give them food, drinks and potty breaks. It depends on how long you would like the promotion to last!

Don't forget about the women! Have a Super Bowl watching party in one room, and next door a *Football Widows* **Party**...women get treated to an entirely free party complete with entertainment and prizes. Make it a great girls day/night out with prizes such as limousine service waiting to take them on an instant shopping spree. Of course, they have to promise to come back at the end of the game to pick up their spouse/friend.   Pamper the women with prizes, such as complete makeovers and facials. If you live in an NFL city, try to get a player from the home team to host it. And, don't forget the male dancers!

Alternatively, to include **married couples**, you can include a lot of listeners involved simultaneously. Get a public location (mall, etc.) and invite married couples to come out and renew their vows. Have a huge, official ceremony followed by a party/reception. Promote it as (your show) wants to give you the chance to tell your spouse that you'd marry her all over again. Give away a 2nd Honeymoon to one of those couples participating.

Here's a great one for an oldies station. Get one of those old **electronic football games** with the vibrating field like you had when you were a kid, and play the two teams against each other. It makes for great audio. That annoying buzz with your reaction! Have listeners call in to offer strategies.

Face it, you're going to have a hard time getting as large a cume during the Super Bowl as usual, but you can promote your own halftime show, just as various TV networks have. Tell listeners to turn down the sound on the TV and listen to your station for some REAL entertainment. Make it big and exciting with a real payoff.

-91-

VALENTINES DAY

The name Saint Valentine is given to two legendary Christian martyrs whose feasts were formerly observed on February 14. It is possible that these two legends were based on real people or, as some believe, one person. The association of Saint Valentine's Day with love and courtship may have arisen from the coincidence of the date with the Roman festival of LUPERCALIA. I

The first publisher of Valentines in the U.S. was Esther Howland, who started a Valentine making business in 1847, which soon grossed over $100,000 a year! Now, of course, it's a multi-million dollar industry for card companies, florists and candy manufacturers.

While these statistics are dated, it is a fair guess that they may still be true. Would you believe that:

- Valentine's for Mothers outsell all others combined by 3 to 1.
- About one-eighth of the flowers sent annually, are sent on this day.
- Roses are by far the number one choice (the rule is: Red roses symbolize love, red tulips symbolize passion).

The X's placed so often on the bottom when signing come from the X often being used by those that could not write as their signature. This practice dates back to the Middle Ages as so few could write. To emphasize sincerity upon "placing their mark" this was often kissed, and conveyed the force of a sworn oath. Since then, the X alone has come to symbolize a kiss at the bottom of a Valentine.

Valentine's Day is growing in profile and importance each year! There are dozens of great ideas to capture the passion of the holiday.

More Valentine's Day information at
www.tjohnsonmedia.com

-92-

VALENTINE'S DAY PROMO IDEAS

In the past decade or so, Valentine's Day has become one of the biggest, most promotable (exploitable) holidays. There are many angles to take, but one that has worked well is the **Broken Hearts Club.** Show sympathy to listeners who don't have a valentine by making them members of your show's "broken hearts club". They win dinner for one, a bouquet of "Forget Me Nots", a single movie ticket, etc. To win, have listeners call when they hear a "Broken Hearts" montage, or have them call and tell you their story of a broken heart. You'll probably find a lot of others who want to "heal" that broken heart, and you may end up with a happy ending! You can even have a Valentine's "Broken Hearts Party", where they all gather and hook up!

It's always a good promotion to offer a free wedding with all expenses paid for the first couple who agrees to **Get Married for Valentine's Day.** Carry the ceremony live on your morning show on Val's day. Pay for the catering, reception, etc. and include a honeymoon trip to a resort location (Hawaii, Jamaica, etc.). Your morning personality could get a ministers' license and perform the ceremony. Visit City Hall to find out how, or look up one of the services on the internet.

Another spin on this idea is to send listeners to Las Vegas to be married in a chapel. There are dozens of wedding chapels there, and they require no blood test. Plan ahead, though. February 14 is the busiest day of the year there. Create a great moment on the air by finding someone who will propose spontaneously on Valentine's Day morning, fly to Vegas and be married by the time you get off the air that morning!

Jeff & Jer have turned the **Mile Of Men** into an annual event in San Diego. Find a public location, hopefully a well-known street in your city. In the week before Valentine's Day, qualify 100 or more available men. Women are then invited out in hopes of meeting the man of their dreams. They cruise down the Mile of Men and select their valentine. When they do, they call the station and claim their man. You send them out on a mass date together that night, and follow up on the 15th with stories about the previous evening.

Hold your own version of the DATING GAME, BLIND DATE or **LOVE CONNECTION** on the morning show all morning long. Winners get a Valentine's Date. These games also translate to a local nightclub well.

Here's another one that will get you on the local television newscasts. Qualify up to 100 couples to gather in public during your morning show for the **Great Kiss Off**. They start kissing and the last one to remain liplocked wins a vacation or other great prizes. If you want to stretch this over several days, allow breaks. If you want to contain it to a day, allow no breaks. It probably won't go more than 12-15 hours, with no pee breaks.

Fill a hot tub with chocolate kisses, displayed in a visible public location, and offer your listeners **Free Kisses**. Listeners donate $2 to a charity to guess how many are in the tub. Closest to actual number wins the hot tub on Val's

There are several online services, and probably some businesses in your town that send dead flowers, moldy candy, etc. to someone that winners want to "get even with". It's a good bit for morning shows. Just work out a trade for mention agreement with the vendor, and send the "gifts" out in exchange for listeners who call you with best "revenge" stories.

GIVEAWAY IDEAS

- ➢ Free baby-sitting for an evening out...perfect if you target adults.
- ➢ Work with a video service and give away video Valentine's to send to those who are far away.
- ➢ A personalized billboard to a listener who has the most romantic or imaginative idea.
- ➢ A bouquet of roses every month for a year, or a rose a day every day for a year.
- ➢ Breakfast in bed, catered by a classy restaurant
- ➢ Victoria's Secret Gift Certificates
- ➢ Massages
- ➢ Make reservations for dinner for guys who forgot. Give away the reservations as prizes for Valentine's Day. It costs you *nothing*!

Day. (the average hot tub holds around 9,000 kisses). You can also "sell" kisses. Have a local group come out and offer kisses for an additional $5 donation!

If you were on the air in the 80s, you probably did this one. Turn your most high profile personality, or maybe your stunt boy, into a **Chocolate Covered DJ.** Start with a giant vat of chocolate, suspend your air talent over the top, and dip them in. The best place to conduct this stunt is usually in a mall, or other high traffic, high visibility location. Ask your listeners to donate to a charity to toss their favorite topping on the jocks. It may be kind of silly, it may be kind of strange, but it does get some attention.

All stunts require a proper set up, but this is one that requires your expertise as well as finding the right couple to make it work. It's called **Seduction.** Find a woman who agrees to dress however she feels sexiest (you pay for whatever she wants at Victoria's Secret) and send her in a limousine to her husband's place of employment. Then, live on the air (and be sure to video tape everything!) capture the moment when she whisks him away to a hotel for a day of pure passion. You may want to clear this with the guy's boss ahead of time. The bit loses a little of the excitement if he loses his job over it!

The city of Verona, Italy is swamped with **letters to Juliet** each year...and they are all answered! Orchestrate a promotion where listeners write letters to Juliet, in care of your station. You read the letters, forward them and distribute the response letters.

-93-

FAST FACTS

- Over the course of a lifetime, how many flowers does the average person give on Valentine's Day? —157.
- According to a recent survey, 45% of American men prefer to make love with the lights on — what percentage of women like it that way? — 17%
- The average woman kisses 79 men before she marries. (according to Dr. Joyce Brothers)
- Did you know a passionate kiss burns up to 12 calories?
- The longest kiss on record lasted 17 days, ten-and-a-half-hours. (it was set in 1985 by a couple in Chicago)
- The average woman thinks about sex once every ten minutes. The average guy thinks about sex once every 2 minutes!
- 76% of married people make it a point to kiss their spouse each day before they leave the house.
- 80% believe their spouses are great kissers. 10% say their mates are duds. The remaining people aren't sure.
- 7 of 10 Americans close their eyes when they kiss, but 61% admit that sometimes they peek.

- 35% said the best kiss of their lives made their knees weak, 33% said they heard fireworks going off, and 23% felt the earth move.
- 41% of us got our first kiss when we were 13 - 15 years old. 36% got theirs between the ages of 16 and 21.

If you are to stand out from the pack, take a different approach. Think outside the box and do things differently.

In planning any promotional activity, be sure to keep in mind the personality of your radio station and the audience you target. That is especially true of Valentine's Day. Shows that target men will approach promotions much differently than those that appeal mostly to women.

-94-

TRIVIA QUIZ

Valentine's Day may not be for you. To find out, take this simple test:

- Saint Valentine is the patron saint of: (a) love, (b) young couples in love, (c) Victoria's Secret, (d) penicillin.
- Complete the following three-word phrase: Valentine's Day _____. (a) card, (b) candy, (c) Massacre, (d) sucks.
- Cupid is in fact: (a) The ancient Roman god of love, (b) Related to the little green sprout in the Green Giant commercial, (c) Gay, (d) Luther Vandross.
- When we say we are lovesick, we really mean that... (a) Infatuation has given us the symptoms of illness, (b) We're pregnant and throw up every morning, (c) Our sexual tastes involve activities that are considered depraved and/or psychotic in most civilized countries, (d) We forgot to practice safe sex.
- According to the Beatle's classic, "All you need is... (a) love, (b) cash, (c) ointment, (d) seldom what you get.
- Sex is most enjoyable when it is done with: (a) someone you cherish, (b) mindless zeal, (c) amyl

nitrate, Crisco and several doorknobs, (d) lots of witnesses.

- Most experts in modern human relations have found that the only two things a man really requires for a fulfilling relationship are: (a) love and trust, (b) friendship and devotion, (c) wealth and good looks, (d) a giant woody and some free time.

Cupid's Helper:
Solicit calls from people having trouble in a rela-
tionship and be the mediator. Or, find someone
who wants to go out with a co-worker but is afraid
to ask. You ask them out on the air for them.

-95-

PHONE TOPICS

Here's a winner every year. Get into the topic creatively, and watch the phones go crazy. "What is the most romantic thing he/she has ever done?". Here are some more winning ideas to involve your audience:

- ➤ Who said the "L" word first?
- ➤ Finish This Poem: "I thought you were my Valentine, but now I'm not so sure."
- ➤ What sayings should be on candy hearts today?
- ➤ Most embarrassing romantic moment.
- ➤ "How we fell in love" stories
- ➤ Calls for best original song or poem about their valentine
- ➤ Weirdest place you've done the wild thing
- ➤ Confessions of past affairs you've had
- ➤ Honeymoon horror stories
- ➤ Strangest "love" story wins prize
- ➤ Sexiest idea for a Valentine's night or weekend wins
- ➤ What is your pet name for each other?
- ➤ Blind Date From Hell stories. The best female blind date story chooses from three male finalists, then they go out on a date with paper bags covering their heads...for the whole evening. Bring them in the following morning to take off the bags on the air.

-96-

St. Patrick's Day

Patrick was the patron saint of Ireland, even though he was not Irish, and, in fact, was born in Britain to a Christian family of Roman citizenship. At the age of 16 he was captured by a marauding horde of Irish and brought back to Ireland, where he was enslaved. Then, after spending 6 years as a herdsman, he managed to escape, returning to the European continent and wandering for several years before joining a monastery. But— after seeing a vision which called him back to Ireland, St. Patrick returned to the emerald Isle and became one of the most successful missionaries in history. And, at the time of his death, Ireland was transformed from a pagan society to one that was almost entirely Christian.

St. Patrick's Day celebrates the anniversary of the death of St. Patrick. The shamrock symbol commemorates his use of the plant to demonstrate the Holy Trinity. There are 166 churches named after St. Patrick in the republic of Ireland.

The stories about St. Patrick and the snakes are conflicting. One myth says he stood atop a mountain named Croagh Patrick and ordered the snakes to leave the country. Another says he beat a drum to scare the reptiles away. There's also a story about a stubborn snake that refused to be driven away. St. Patrick made a box and tried to persuade the snake to get in it. When he slithered in, St. Patrick immediately shut the lid and threw the box into the ocean.

A leprechaun is less than 24 inches tall, dresses in bright colors and is skilled as a shoemaker. If you surprise him, he might lead you to his pot of gold. Your best chance of seeing one will come if you visit one too many pubs.

There are several stories about leprechauns.One Irish myth claims that if worn shoes are placed outside your house, leprechauns would repair them.

Leprechauns were once part of a group known as Luchorpan, or "wee ones." Shoemakers in that time usually lived alone and were grumpy, so leprechauns, who were rich and bad tempered, were depicted as loners. The story goes that if you captured and kept your eye on a leprechaun, he couldn't vanish. And often he would tell his captor the location of his pot of gold as a ransom.

Another story tells of a tricky leprechaun who was caught in a field. The leprechaun told the man who caught him that a certain pot of gold was buried under a weed in a field. The man tied a red handkerchief to the weed and left to get his shovel. When he returned, the leprechaun had tied red handkerchiefs to all the weeds in the field.

As for the Blarney Stone: Blarney Castle in Limerick, Ireland, was spared from destruction by the English when an Irishman convinced the English not to destroy it. Since all the other castles were destroyed, the people in Limerick said the Irishman "kissed the Blarney Stone" and received good luck.

GIVE AWAY IDEAS:

Anything Green, such as:

> Bottles of Cloraseptic
> Irish Spring Soap
> Palmolive dish soap
> Notre Dame memorabilia (Fighting Irish),
> Shamrocks
> Lucky Charms
> Boston Celtics tickets

Get a copy of the movie "Leprechaun" for some great drops...also record some LUCKY CHARMS commercials from TV (Always after me Lucky Charms)

-97-

IRISH HUMOR

You could fill your St. Patrick's Day show entirely with Irish jokes. Just open the phones and take the calls! Here are a couple to get you started. You can get a bunch more just by modifying   other ethnic jokes, blonde jokes, etc.

- If I wasn't Irish, know what I'd rather be? Dead
- Me boy, there are only 2 kinds of people in the world, those who are Irish, and those who wish they were.
- A dentist, young doctor Malone, got a charming girl patient alone. And in his depravity, he filled the wrong cavity. And my how his practice has grown!
- What's an Irish chauffer-driven limousine called? A Paddy wagon.
- "Tell me, O'Callaghan", asked the Priest, "would you like yourself to be buried in a Protestant graveyard?" "Not me, Father" replied the man, "I'd rather die first!"
- How do Irish brain cells die? Alone.
- How do you measure an Irishman's intelligence? Stick a tire pressure gauge in his ear!

-98-

IRISH BLESSINGS

Here's a great St. Patrick's Day call-in feature. Ask your listeners to call in with their best "Irish Blessings"...seed the pump with things like these:

- May the wind be at your back, especially if you're relieving yourself at the time..
- May some one actually pay attention when your car alarm goes off.
- May Oprah never be allowed to talk about her weight loss, to save us from all the those Skinny-Fat shows.
- May the Surgeon General never allow cigarette companies to disclose the true contents of their product.
- May the leprechaun get you out of your next appointment with IRS.
- May you never be caught copying down the phone number of the Anal Wart Removal Clinic.
- May kissing the blarney stone bring you luck. Kissing your boss's butt guarantees it.
- May you enjoy the finer things of the Leprechaun, except being small in the wrong places.
- May the green on your sleeve be more than left overs from last week's cold.

IRISH DAY IDEAS

One cup of **Irish coffee** provides four essential food groups: Alcohol, caffeine, sugar and fat! How about making the world's largest Irish Coffee...a hot tub full of coffee and Bailey's.

Find a **bagpipe player a**nd have him on the air, or at least record some station jingles for the day.

Fill a hot tub with various denominations of small bills, including $1, $5 and $10 for the **Rollin' o' the Green**. A winner gets a chance to cover themselves with green honey and roll in the hot tub...any money that sticks...they keep!

Have the morning show petition the mayor to make all traffic lights in the city green all day long.

If you have a trivia feature, make it **Green Trivia**. All answers have "Green" included. Greenpeace, Green Bay Packers, Green House Effect, Greenland, Mr. Green Jeans, Green Hornet, etc.

Invite listeners to call in and **get their "Irish" up**. They call in and get 10 seconds to sound off at whatever makes them mad. The most creative, best one each hour is played on the air and given a small prize.

Listeners have to talk in an **Irish Brogue** all morning. If they don't, you disconnect them, or throw them off the air. Weave it into your entire show. And, everyone who calls gets an O'- in front of their name. O'Bob, O'Sharon.

Build the world's largest **Corned Beef Sandwich**. Invite listeners to come and eat it (free of course) at your St. Pat's Party.

From the Desk of...Marilyn Monroe

"It's not true that I had nothing on. I had the radio on."

-Marilyn responding to posing nude for a calendar in 1957

-99-

APRIL FOOL'S DAY

April Fool's Day offers your station a chance to put some much-needed (and often neglected) *fun* into your morning show, and into your station. All worthwhile April Fool's gags require some brainstorming and planning, as well as great execution. You should plan for some complaint calls from listeners who fall victim to your bit. After all, some listeners just don't have a sense of humor. However, be careful to pull off your ideas with good taste and in synch with your overall station image and profile. No matter how great the joke is, it's not worth damaging your reputation or image!

When planning your April 1 activity, remember the FCC has very strict guidelines about airing obscene material and on-air hoaxes, or the broadcast of false or deceptive programming. Their motive is to help you uphold the trust that the public places in a broadcaster.

As simple as knowingly giving the incorrect time during the morning show can cause complaints and potentially cause public harm. The FCC guidelines seek to insure that hoaxes do not pose a threat to the public's safety and welfare.

There are cases involving investigation of programming and promotion departments at radio stations for deceptive broadcasting. The rule applies to advertisements and news as well. Creative April Fools programming should be well conceived and carefully planned with the renewed focus of the FCC and the possibility of serious sanctions.

If you are in doubt as to the legality of your idea, be sure to check with station management and/or your legal counsel.

Pulling off a stunt for April Fool's Day can be as simple as a self-contained gag that airs on your show, or as complex as something that takes over the entire station. The most important thing is to plan your pranks creatively, and go for something that works *on the air*. Giving out the wrong time may screw up listener's lives and create talk, but it's not much fun to listen to, and mostly achieves the questionable objective of making your show sound stupid!

The *best* bits are those that have "legs". It may take a few days of teasing and set-up, but that's even better in pulling off the good-natured deception! The audience won't see it coming.

You should also be careful to not tell *anyone* that it's a joke, unless they are in a position that requires their participation. If the rest of the staff is duped along with your listeners, you know that they won't "blow" the joke for you.

Here are some good ideas, ranging from the simple to the complex. Good luck, and have fun!

The Garage Door Opener

Broadcast a tone that, "according to our engineer" will open many garage doors. Have neighbors and friends of yours lined up to testify that when they turned up the radio in the garage "Sure enough, the door opened!" You, of course, will prove this by playing the tone while they are in the garage as they hit the button and have the door going up and down. Be creative with this and come up with different ways you "plan to use this throughout the day".

Half-Off Sale

Announce that the government is offering 50% off specials on all back taxes, fines and jail time. It's perfect timing with the tax deadline approaching, and money being tight right now. Again, set up some calls claiming that it works! Note: check with legal!

Bag your phone

This is a classic! To work right, you must set it up and pre-sell it 1-3 days in advance. Run liners, news stories and/or fake commercials explaining that the phone company is cleaning out the phone lines in your area. If you can, find actual phone company reps (legal warning: don't say the *name* of your local phone company...just say "phone company") to come on the air explaining the procedure and that "dust and dirt could come through the phone, which lowers the quality of the transmission. And, we're preparing upgrades to all of the service in our area". The listeners are asked to "put all your phones in a plastic bag". This is to avoid having the dust and dirt blow out through their phone lines and soil their homes. Have setup "listeners" calling in to give you reports of what happened at their homes when they forgot to bag their phone.

Bag Your Phone Variations

There are a few variations on the "bag your phone" theme, and you can probably think of a lot more applications. Here are a couple of spin-offs:

1. Tell listeners the water company has called saying the hot water has been turned off, due to possible contamination. The public is advised to use only cold water until further notice.

2. Convince listeners they need to close their toilet lid and put something heavy on it since the water company is planning to "back up the lines" and open toilets could explode with sewage.

3. Announce a problem with sewer rats coming up through the toilets. All listeners are instructed to flush their toilets at 7:55 am to flush out the problem and to cover the bowl with Saran Wrap "in case water backed up."

Beer Truck:

Get on the air talking about the Beer Truck that's turned over on it's side, and how they can't tow it until they unload the beer. The beer company (again, don't say the name of the company) has said it's cheaper to just give the beer away, than it would be to switch out trucks and haul it off. So you give the location of the truck on the air, and tell everyone that the limit is 6 cases per person. Do a few updates and let everyone know the progress of the "beer truck." Include information that the driver is not from around here (so no-one will worry about their husbands) and how no one is hurt. You may want to have your promotion staff on site waiting with prizes for the listeners who come out. A promotion guaranteed to bring out the Homer Simpsons in your audience!

Free Money?

The setup is simple: A local billionaire (you make up the name) has passed away. He has put it in his will to give everyone within the city limits $500.00. If you would like to get your share, you must call a number, or go to a specific location. Of course, the number is a "disconnect" and the location doesn't exiist.

Free Plastic Surgery

Offer free plastic surgery to the first xxx people to show up at a certain location. The only catch is that they have to accept whatever surgery is chosen by spinning a wheel. It's hilarious on the air. Do the entire show complete with doctors and lots of live atmosphere. Believe it or not, people will show up!

The Flying Cat Circus

Here's one that will guarantee an emotional response from the animal rights activists and cat lovers in your town. Announce that the famous Russian Flying Cats Circus is coming to town. Produce spots that promote cats starring in various outrageous stunts such as being thrown out of an airplane, set on fire, shot from a cannon, etc. use your imagination and be creative. But make the spot sound like a real commercial. Try to give away tickets to this thing. The animal rights people will love it-not.

Pet Taxes.

This one is pretty easy. Just run announcements all day long that your listeners can beat the new, coming Pet Tax by doing something you ask them to. The more outrageous, the better.

Sound Sensor Traffic Lights

This is a great one that is also easy to execute. YOUR TOWN is one of the new test cities for the new "sound sensor traffic lights". If you pull up to an intersection with a red light and there is no traffic coming from either way, you can honk your horn twice and the traffic light will change the red light to a green light. Listeners will call and swear that it works, or that it is broken. If listeners say it doesn't work, ask them type of car they are driving, have them honk for you, suggest that their horn isn't loud enough, or try and convince them they honked too long or too short, etc.

Format Change

Warning: Don't try this one unless you have a station that is very well known and entrenched in your market. Otherwise, you'll simply confuse the audience. Even then, the value of a stunt like this is questionable, but it may work for you. The idea is to change format without changing positioning statements or programming elements. Start playing all polka or all 70's, etc. Keep introducing your current music list but play different titles.

Other twists during the show or day:

- Change newscasts to news from a different era.

- Keep your same format, but the YEAR is different. You'll be introducing NEW songs that are 10 years old, announcing the debut of movies from that year, etc.

WGCI-FM/Chicago kicked morning man Steve Harvey off the air and announced it was switching to "The New 107-5 WGCI, All Reggae, All The Time." Club mixer (and Belize-native) Steve Maestro turned on his Caribbean accent and became "Basil St. John" for the morning. PD Elroy Smith said some listeners were happy about the switch.

You don't have to change formats to have the same effect. Adult Alternative KXPK/Denver morning members Pete MacKay and Mari Szatkowski recruited foreign-language students from local colleges to do commercials, breaks, and such in Chinese, Arabic, French, Russian, and German.

New Subway

All morning long, you're offering to give away free rides on the new (your town's) subway. Of course there isn't one.

For added impact, broadcast the show "live" from the new subway. Use plenty of sound effects and theater of the mind. You can even invite listeners to the new subway station, and when they show up, give away free subway sandwiches

Taking the same idea, you can announce the grand opening of a new underground mall, complete with waterslide and roller coaster. Do setup "live broadcasts".

Burn Your Buns!

This is a great prank to play on a member of your morning show, or have one of your listeners play on a friend. This can get your audience involved vicariously through your listener's world. Take home some hotel stationery. Prepare a package with a man's tie, a teddy and a bra to somebody's boss' home. A nice letter from the manager is included saying that housekeeping found the items after he checked out. Wow!

Or, find someone willing to go to a large department store and find the basket next to the cash register where the clerk puts those plastic security tabs. After someone completes their purchase, drop one in each bag and watch/listen as the unsuspecting customer heads out the door through the security stystem!

Fun at the Restaurant

It's always fun to fool around with another person's food order, but be prepared to spend a little money because this one will cost you. Find someone who has a friend who loves a good rare steak. After placing their order, the prankster heads for the kitchen. Have the chef cook that bad boy so that it resembles a used wallet. Have him leave the red "rare" marker in the steak and serve it. You'll have to pay for two dinners to get this done, but the reaction on the air is well worth it! Once dinner is served just sit back and watch the show. Ask the waiter to do his part by avoiding your table immediately after serving your dinners, and being difficult when the victim complains.

Trading Places

A few years ago, L.A. Mayor Richard Riordan and Rick Dees traded places for a few hours. This is a high profile exchange that used April 1 as a means of generating a little publicity for both parties and doesn't require any attempt at fooling the audience. In fact, you can promote it. At KIIS, while the mayor spun CDs from Alanis Morissette at KIIS's Burbank studios, Dees rested his feet on the mayor's desk a few miles away at City Hall.

Another alternative is to find another station in town, and swap your jocks for theirs. Trading Country jocks with Top 40 can be hilarious, if both morning shows participate in the right spirit. With consolidation, it should be easier to find a willing partner for this.

Suspend the Morning Show

You can develop some sympathy, empathy, attention and passion for the morning show if one of the "suits" from the station fires, suspends or simply removes the show for some reason. In fact, it may be even more effective to have the station manager take their place on the air and take calls about the discipline. The manager refuses to go into detail about what happened or why, and is vague about the details. This will create a public outrage and listeners will demand the show be re-instated. They return triumphantly to the air the following morning. It's up to you whether you let the audience in on whether or not it is a prank or not!

Aroma Therapy Reaches a New Level

WGHT/Pompton Lakes, NJ got some press when they began airing elaborately produced promos a week before April Fools Day, telling listeners they had developed the technology to transmit aromas — called"Aroma-Mod" — over the airwaves. Listeners were spotted around town putting their noses to the dashboards of their cars, and one caller said he detected cinnamon-apple muffins emanating from his speaker! You can build this over time and take it to whatever extent you can dream up. This can be brilliant with the right execution.

Promoting Locally

If you have a large local issue that you can tap into, you may be able to generate a lot of attention. WZTA/Miami personalities Ron Brewer and Paul Castronovo once announced that they were able to arrange for Fidel Castro to come to Miami for a visit and that Gloria Estefan was hosting him for dinner. The station said listeners were happy and excited to hear the news.

Many stations have gotten attention by making announcements surrounding their sports teams. KKRZ/Portland morning drivers John Murphy and Dan Clarke received lots of media attention in the Pacific Northwest after announcing Microsoft co-founder (and Portland Trailblazers owner) Paul Allen had struck a deal to purchase and move the unhappy Seattle Seahawks NFL franchise to Portland. Other stations have announced the trade of their city's most popular sports star!

Again, proceed cautiously with a bit like these. Like the boy who cried "wolf", you run the risk of not being taken seriously in the future.

Spectacle in the Sky

Announce that the Hale-Bopp comet and an asteroid labeled Lirpa 1 (April 1 backwards) are on a collision course which will result in a spectacular light show in broad daylight at noon. Stand with your back to the sun, facing north and looking straight up. Use a filter GREN NO. 4102 plastic or glass. 41xx is the industry number for colors (of course that is also the date). It's the same green you find in a Sprite bottle or a Rolling Rock bottle. If you look through these bottles, the filter will diffuse the rays. Bring in experts from a non-existent Astronomy department, etc. to enhance the bit.

The Bit That Never Was

Sometime in your first half hour play a pre-recorded break done by the GM or OM or a lawyer or somebody of importance saying that the station apologizes for the remarks made by the morning show and that at ??o'clock a deposition will begin to find out exactly what happened. Have them say the morning show had made an attempt at a gag for April Fool's Day and that they had offended a large amount of people. From there, have "listeners" standing by wanting to know what you did. Of course you can't repeat any of it because it was so tasteless. Let the excitement rage all morning. The gag is that you never said *anything* off-color. It's a great way to gain the image of having an edge without doing *anything at all.*

No Smoking

On April Fools Day, announce that a new law has gone into effect immediately that makes it illegal to smoke in your vehicle. Run the entire story first in every newscast as well (Note: If you take your news image seriously, you may want to avoid this step). To add credibility, say the Governor enacted the law because of disturbing information he received from the American Cancer Society. It said that because many drivers were smoking, lighting cigarettes, or dropping lit cigarettes in their laps while driving and not paying attention, that too many accidents are attributed to in-car smoking. The fines were $50 for the first offense, $150 for the second and $500 and/or jail time for the third offense. Set up fake calls from people saying that they got busted on the way to work.

Quick, Easy Ideas

If you have decided to NOT do a major April Fool joke on the air, here are some ideas that you can use to still capture the day on the air with your audience:

- Announce free prizes all morning at a public location that doesn't exist, such as the corner of ___ and ____. The trick is that those streets are close together, but run parallel.

- Tell listeners your morning show is being simulcast on Channel 77 (or any other unused channel).

- Broadcast from a nonexistent location, such as an intersection that doesn't exist. You're out there giving away lots of great, valuable prizes.

- Give away $500,000 ... $1 a year for 500,000 years!

- Play selections of novelty hits from past. Dr. Demento has a lot of "fool-ish" songs.

- Stop people on the street and offer them the chance to take a cream pie in the face. They choose between two pies, one with a small amount of money ($10), the other with a large prize ($100).

- Take calls from listeners on April Fool jokes they have played or been victim of

- Pick a little known "fact" that could be true or false.

Listeners call in to decide if you're "fooling" or not. If they are correct, they win. For a twist, give 3-4 statements, and the listener must identify the false one.

- Hold your own April Fools' Parade...name it something silly, or just invite people who want to be April Fools to come and join you. Your morning show can announce the parade on the air, complete with sound effects, describing the floats, etc. This requires a lot of production and pre-planning, but it can be effective theater of the mind!

- Every 10 minutes or so, play the sound effect of a cell phone start ringing on the air. Let it ring 4-5 times, then stop. Never say anything about it, and don't acknowledge it at all. It'll drive listeners crazy (thinking it is theirs).

How important is production value in pulling off APRIL fool's Day bits? Think about some of your favorite songs and how inane the lyrics are (Shake Your Booty, MacArthur Park, Karma Chameleon, etc). Yet when put to music, the lyrics come alive. Lyrics are the content...the melody is the production value...and the magic is provided by the performer.

-100-

TAX DAY

There are only two things that are certain, and this is one of them. The other, as you know, is death. Tax Day (April 15), is an opportunity for some minor promotions and it usually provides some good morning show content.

On April 15, hire an IRS Agent to sit in a **Dunk Tank** at the main post office location, local mall, etc. Tax filers get a free (or donation to charity) shot to dunk the IRS. At the same event, get an old white refrigerator, paint it like a 1040 form, and have people take shots at it with a sledgehammer.

Stuff a piñata with "your tax refund". Listeners take their best shot at the **IRS Pinata,** shaking the money loose out of the piñata.

Become the station or show where IRS stands for Instant Refund Station. Winners can spin the **Wheel of Refunds** to win cash and a new station T-shirt, since the IRS stole the "shirt off your back".

Give away headache remedies and advice from a tax consultant. It's even more effective when you offer that last-second tax advice on April 15. Listeners come by and get their tax kits from you, and your expert looks over their

A great comedy drop to air on tax day is Steve Martin's bit from "Comedy Is Not Pretty"...it's called "You Can Be A Millionaire"

return. An added twist is to give away a **Tax Relief Free For All** getaway (plane tickets to somewhere nice).

Give a listener a ticket to anywhere outside the US for Tax Day to send your audience **On the Lam from Uncle Sam**. The idea is that if you are out of the country on tax day, you get an automatic extension. The law has changed in recent years, but the promotion can still be done. In addition to an airline ticket to a foreign location, give the listener an IRS extension form.

Did you cheat on your taxes? Really! Have listeners call and change their names to Bob or Linda, and tell you the juicy details.

A variation is to have raw Easter Eggs to throw at the IRS Agent. There-you can address two holidays at once.

If you're getting tax stuff together remember these items are not tax deductible:

➢ Even if you always drink to people's health, don't deduct liquor as a medical expense.

➢ Toupees and hair weaves are not considered overhead.

➢ Bras cannot be deducted as upkeep.

➢ Cigarettes can not be listed under "loss by fire."

➢ Laxatives and high fiber cereal can't be included in "moving expenses."

-101-

EASTER

It's easy to have fun with Easter. Just get some eggs and use your imagination. They're a lot of fun when they explode in a microwave!

Here's an easy warm and fuzzy. Just rent a **Bunny Costume** and go to any area where there are kids, especially if you visit hospitals to deliver treats to sick kids. But before you return the bunny costume, put a microphone inside the bunny "head" and send the bunny out in the community as if it were a real person on the commute. Dress in a business suit and stand in line for coffee, buy a newspaper, ride the bus, etc. You can get some great audio from those nearby.

Dress up an otherwise typical egg hunt just by creating a **$100 Egg** and hiding it somewhere in town. Give clues. Put a certificate inside—not actual cash—that way the winner has to come to the station. For fun, drop some other eggs with "a wrong-egg" message inside. Keep everything in "plain sight" and on public property. This could make for a station weekend promotion.

Get your stunt person to go around with a basket full of Easter eggs. Tell people that one of them is raw—the rest are hard-boiled. They must select one and slam it against their forehead. If it's hard-boiled, they win a prize. Of course, NONE of them are hard-boiled. Everybody gets a prize any way.

It's the **raw egg drop**. Take a dozen eggs and drop them from atop a large building...at least one story up. Listeners bring any device they want to try and catch them. Award prizes for those that succeed in catching one out of three eggs. Have a larger prize for the "champion".

An **Easter Egg Toss** is simple, and it's fun. Get two lines of listeners facing each other. They toss eggs to each other, and the last pair with an unbroken egg wins. Keep moving them further back after each successful "catch".

Hint: The best device I know of to catch these is several pair of panty hose sewn together to form a "basket".

Easter Egg Golfing is fun too! Take along some of your hard-boiled and decorated Easter Eggs, to a miniature golf course. Listeners have to putt the eggs into the hole for prizes. Or, take a bucket of eggs to a driving range and let listeners come out and tee off. For grins, put in a couple of raw eggs!

This makes for a good, quick bit on a show. Solicit 3-5 listeners willing to compete to see who can **eat the most boiled eggs** in 15 minutes. This *sounds* easy, but it's NOT!

Here's a good stunt that may get you on TV. Find some bald guys (need to be clean shaven) to join you for an **Easter Egghead coloring contest**. They decorate their OWN head like an Easter egg. Let your contestants bring their own stuff to use.

TONS of Easter ideas for morning shows are online at tjohnsonmedia.com

-102-

SECRETARY'S DAY

We've come a long way in the last couple of decades, which makes this one of the trickier days to relate to. The word "secretary" isn't politically correct anymore, but those "executive assistants" are still expecting to be honored, or at least taken to lunch.

The days of conducting **Office Olympics**, featuring competitions in events like chair racing, shooting wastepaper baskets, speed typing, etc. are long gone. It's the same with the old Typewriter Toss (does anyone have a typewriter anymore?). But you can still get some mileage out of the day. Here are some ideas:

Get the Mayor's, Congressman's or other semi-famous person's secretary on the phone for a short interview. Have listeners ask yes/no questions to guess **Whose Secretary Am I?** If they guess correctly, they win.

What do secretaries *really* want for secretaries' Day? **Male Dancers.** Send male strippers out to their office, or have a big party just for secretaries. They win their tickets on the air.

Fill a plane with bosses and have the secretaries **Toss The Boss** out. There are plenty of parachute schools "dying" to get on the air! It's a perfect fantasy fulfillment for your female audience!

Set up tables inside an empty swimming pool, and have a party for secretaries inside the **Secretarial "Pool"**. It's perfect for hotels that have not yet filled their outdoor pool, but you are dependent upon the weather.

Have office workers fax in nominations for good secretaries, then go out with the spokesperson for the local Professional Florists Association and literally **Bury Your Secretary** in her workspace with hundreds of flowers. This makes a good picture for TV or the newspaper.

Get two secretaries on the line and tell them to have a pen and note pad handy. Then tell them to answer the phone as if they were at work and **Take A Message.** They have to dictate the following message that you give them. Read quickly: "Hi, this is Bob Billings from Billings, not Bill Bowling from Boston. Im coming in on Flight 487 which was 574 before we made a stop in Biscayne and switched to Flight 487. I have the Tornado Tool account, but not the Tiny Teeth Charts. Those are coming with Bill Billings from Boston. I mean Bill Bowling. If you could tell your boss that Bob and Bill will have both accounts for him next Tuesday after the first of the month, not the previous Thursday from which we previously spoke. Have a nice day!" Have them recite the message back to you, the secretary with the most information correct wins!

Have a contest and ask the listeners to **Name the TV Bosses.** You give a list of bosses from TV shows and they have to fax back the secretaries:

- ➢ Maggie Hayes, Miss DiPesto
- ➢ Mr. Drysdale, Jane Hathaway
- ➢ WKRP In Cincinnati, Jennifer Marlowe

Three Great Phone Topics

1. What is the stupidest thing your boss has ever done?

2. What is the most embarrassing thing that has happened to you as a secretary? Offer to electronically alter voices to encourage more calls.

3. Is getting flowers at work from your boss inappropriate? You give flowers to people who you're intimate with, or who you love deeply, and your mother. But getting them from your boss? Is it creepy?

At Star 100.7/San Diego, Jagger & Kristi host an annual Secretary's Day "Bootie Cruise" featuring male dancers. IT sells out very quickly each year.

-103-

MOTHER'S DAY

Moms come equipped with the wisdom to know that by the time a child of any age asks, it is often too late for the answer to be of help.

This is one of those great Holidays that allow for tremendous emotional and fun moments.

Put together a prize package for the **Best Single Mom.** Kids e-mail or write why their single mom is the best. Read some of the entries on the air and then call the mom to tell them what their little one said about them. Single moms are real heroes!

Take calls offering several rounds of **Dueling Moms**. Get two moms on the line. Ask questions like, "What do you feed your sick child?" Once you get past chicken noodle soup there aren't a whole lot of things immediately associated with helping someone get well. It's fun listening to two otherwise sane mothers saying they'd feed their sick children cheese doodles and ho-ho's.

Give away a limo for a day (any day she chooses) for **Mother's Day Out**, a complete makeover with massage, $500 clothing trade, dinner at elegant restaurant, daycare for children for the day, etc. Use a mail or fax method with

A full library of Mother's Day ideas are available online at tjohnsonmedia.com

people writing in 25 words or less why their mom is the best.

Go to local elementary schools and record children sending their mom a Mother's Day message. Send home a note with the kids telling their moms to listen for their children on the air the week before Mother's Day-guaranteed to spike parental listening that week! Call it **My Mom is Great**. Produce them with intro/outro.

Female personalities that have children should **Bring Kids to Work** to be on the air with them the Friday before Mother's Day. Another twist is for all jocks to bring their mother in as guest DJ for the Friday. Have them tell stories about the jock when they were kids, etc.

Ask listeners to call their mom and say sappy things to **Make Your Mother Cry**. Or, be funny and get them to ask "why are you calling" in order to win.

A great phone topic is asking listeners something they did and got away with. Then call and **Confess To Your Mom** on the air.

Listeners have to play the **Mother Match Game**, where they are asked questions such as "When do you think your mom lost her virginity?", "Which boyfriend/girlfriend was your mom's favorite?"

The book "MOMILIES" by Michelle Slung is available at bookstores. It is a list of things mom's typically say (Don't run with scissors, etc.)

Can't miss Phone Topics

What's the stupidest, silliest, most embarrassing thing your mom has ever done?

What is your mother's strangest habit?

What is the most unusual meal your mom makes?

What secrets have you kept from your mom?

What's the best/worst advice your mom ever gave you?

What TV mom would you like to have?

Entries from "Mom's Dictionary"

➢ Apple: Nutritious lunchtime dessert which kids trade for cupcakes

➢ Bathroom: A room used by the entire family, believed by all except Mom to be self cleaning.

➢ Bed and Breakfast: Two things kids will never make for themselves.

➢ Lake: A large body of water into which a kid will jump should his friends do so.

➢ Milk: A healthful beverage which kids will gladly drink once it's turned into junk food by the addition of sugar and cocoa.

➢ Open: The position of kids mouths when they eat in front of company.

-104-

MEMORIAL DAY WEEKEND

Memorial Day is the "unofficial" start of summer, bookendinig with Labor Day for the season of fun!

B y federal law, Memorial Day is now celebrated the last Monday in May. The origins of Memorial Day, or decoration day as it was first known, are remote and mixed. In rural America, the custom of cleaning the cemeteries and decorating graves, usually in late summer, was an occasion for reunions, revivals, and picnics.

Memorial day, at the beginning of summer, like labor day at its end, is a convenient open space on the calendar for less somber events, and has become a traditional time for family cookouts in the backyard or sporting events like the Indianapolis 500.

Since the holiday is always on a Monday, and your show will likely be off that day (if you're working, you need to re-negotiate your contract), there isn't a whole lot you can do on the morning show. But there are some opportunities to cash in promotionally and if you have too much energy (and no life), your show may be able to score some extra points with listeners by going out and meeting potential listeners.

Plan to be very visible. The obvious things are visiting the

Don't miss the Memorial Day promotion ideas and morning show content for SUMMER online at tjohnsonmedia.com

parks and handing out prizes at the beach, picnics, or wherever your listeners may gather. Many stations send out prize patrols all day long!

Or, you may choose to celebrate the beginning of summer with some of the following ideas:

- ➢ Give away cookouts, picnics, etc.
- ➢ Give away backyard barbecues complete with grill, burgers, soda, beer, etc.
- ➢ Tie in grocery stores and give away barbecue packs consisting of hot dogs, hamburgers, potato salad, etc. Then, have jocks personally deliver the prize packages to winners on Memorial Day
- ➢ Pool patrol. Don't forget large apartment complexes. Give away prizes such as soda, sun tan lotion, Frisbees, beach balls, beach towels, etc.
- ➢ Trigger prize giveaways by listening for the sound of the roller coaster, or other local summer-oriented sound. Remember, this is theater of the mind, and your production elements can help you tap into the summer mindset. Winners can receive passes and tickets good for local amusement and water parks, outdoor theaters, etc.
- ➢ Give away pools with your station logo on the bottom. Kids' pools, wading pools, all the way up to a full installation of an in-ground pool.
- ➢ Don't forget the beaches. Maybe you should stake out a huge part of a popular beach and throw a giant beach party with water games and contests, live bands, lip synch contests, karaoke, limbo, best bikini, etc.

Memorial Day weekend is the time of many new movie releases. Make contacts with local theaters to get tickets to give away!

-105-

PROM

The younger the demographic makeup of your audience, the more involved you will be in prom season. Whether you target teens or their parents, though, you will want to deal with this time of the year in some fashion, even if it's something as simple as congratulating schools with on-air mentions and students celebrating graduation/end of school, etc.

.

Organize a public service campaign against drunk driving **Prom Promise**, a pledge card not to drink and drive on prom night, but to call home instead. The school with the most returned cards wins a free concert at the school, or a free ALL NIGHT after-prom party at the school sponsored by the station)..

➢ Tie in with local cab company for free rides home from parties.

➢ Give away limo service, tux rentals, corsages, etc. as prizes. Call it a complete prom package.

You'll sound like a real HERO if you find a guy or girl in your audience who is not going to prom because he she doesn't have a date. You provide the **Dating Service.** Showcase their personalities and match them up with someone who takes them to the prom and makes a lifetime memory! Or, have one of the members of your show be their date! It may get you some TV.

Prom Costs

Investigate how much it costs in YOUR town to go to the prom. The national average continues to skyrocket, and in some areas it is up to about $3,000 per couple.

My Prom

Finally, here's an emotional poem written from the perspective of a teenager about drinking and driving. Use this, edit it, rewrite it, produce it with appropriate background music. It's powerful. It gets attention.

I went to a party, mom, I remembered what you said.
You told me not to drink, mom, so I drank Coke instead.
I felt really proud inside, mom, the way you said I would.
I didn't drink and drive, mom, even though others said I should.
I know I did the right thing, mom, I know you're always right.
Now the party is finally ending, mom, as everyone drives out of sight.
As I got into my car, mom, I knew I'd get home in one piece,
Because of the way you raised me, mom, so responsible and sweet.

I started driving away, mom, but as I pulled onto the road,
The other car didn't see me, mom, and it hit me like a load.
As I lie here on the pavement, mom, I hear the policeman say
The other guy is drunk, mom, and now I'm the one who'll pay.
I'm lying here dying, mom, I wish you'd get here soon.
How come this happened to me, mom? My life burst like a balloon.

There is blood all around me, mom, and most of it is mine.
I hear the paramedic say, mom, I'll die in a very short time.
I just wanted to tell you, mom, I swear I didn't drink.
It was the others, mom, the others didn't think.

He didn't know where he was going, mom, he was at the same party as I.
The only difference is, mom, he drank and I will die.
Why do people drink, mom? It can ruin your whole life.
I'm feeling sharp pains now, mom, pains just like a knife.
The guy who hit me is walking, mom, I don't think that's fair.
I'm lying here dying, mom, while all he can do is stare.

Tell my brother not to cry, mom, tell daddy to be brave.
And when I get to heaven, mom, write "daddy's girl" on my grave.
Someone should have told him, mom, not to drink and drive.
If only they would have taken time, mom, I would still be alive.
My breath is getting shorter, mom, I'm becoming very scared.
Please don't cry for me, mom, because when I needed you, you were always there.
I have one last question, mom, before I say goodbye.
I didn't ever drink, mom, so why am I to die?

How To Tell It's Going To Be A Rotten Prom

10. You pick up your rented tux, go home and try it on, and you realize it has a rabbit in the breast pocket and the lapels squirt water.

9. Your limo driver has to call his probation officer for permission to leave the "House Arrest Zone."

8. Your date arrives and your Dad answers the door in his underwear.

7. In your hurry to get ready, you mistakenly grab a can of rustoleum instead of hairspray.

6. You're still in a hurry to get ready and brush your teeth with Preparation H.

5. One of the old teachers chaperoning drops her dentures in the punch bowl.

4. The booking agency mistakenly sends a square dance band.

3. The theme of the prom is "Bosnian Relief Now."

2. The prom sight has been double-booked and you have to wait three hours until the VFW dance is over.

1. The "surprise band" takes the stage and you find out it's "The New Carpenters."

-106-

FATHER'S DAY

F ather's Day is not *nearly* as big a deal as Mother's Day. But there are still some ideas worth considering the week leading up to the occasion.

By far, the best idea I've ever heard is Jeff & Jer's annual **Father's Day Reunion** feature. About 2-3 weeks prior, they solicit listeners who have been separated from their father for a long time and don't know where he is. Many of the respondents have *never* met their father. Working with a private detective that specializes in finding missing persons, they track down one father who agrees to fly to be on the morning show the Friday before Father's Day. That morning, the listener is brought to the station expecting to make a phone call to talk to their father for the first time. The emotional reaction when the father walks in and is introduced to their child is priceless. Television cameras capture every moment!

Fly everyone in the family to one location to be together with dad for an entire **Family Reunion**.

At the **Mr. Dad Pageant**, you bring dads on stage in bathrobes, drinking beer, scratching themselves etc. set up in a similar format to Miss America. You could have a dance contest, butt-crack/blue jeans competition, formal

If you can't find what you're looking for here, check out more Father's Day ideas online at tjohnsonmedia.com

wear competition (same jeans, but t-shirt is tucked in), talent contest (excuses for not shaving, belching, etc), trivia questions based on sports, etc.

Recognizing that one of the most dreaded phrases father's ever see, **Some Assembly Required,** this feature can be hilarious on the air. Kids solicit their fathers in a bike-building contest. The father's race to build the bike, first one finished (with child cheering in background) wins the bike. Do it without giving them the instructions! Unknown to the loser is that they will also get the bike. Good press for TV. OR-Get 5 gas grills. Solicit 5 contestants. They each get the recommended tools for assembling the grill... but again, you keep the instructions. The first dad to assemble the grill, and make fire, wins.

Take single mothers and kids on an activity that is usually reserved for fathers. You act as **Surrogate Father.** It's great for some "warm and fuzzy" image building. Plan fishing trips, baseball games, etc. A "Big Brother" image may be good for your morning show.

You provide power tools, and something that needs to be constructed. The dad who puts it together fastest wins in the **Power Tool Showdown** . The catch is that there's a whining, nagging woman yakking at them the entire time!

Just like "Name that TV Mom", you can play **Name That TV Dad**. You give the TV show, they name the dad.

Day after phone bit: What did you want? What did you get?

-107-

SUMMERTIME!

You can use many of these ideas in your Memorial Day programming, but here are some more ideas to tap into that "summer" lifestyle and mindset.

As we get into the heat of the summer months, review everything you do on your show, your station and all of your promotional plans for the rest of the year. Are you doing everything you can to reach your audience where they are this summer? Does your station and your morning show *sound* like summer? (And no, that doesn't mean that it should sound like you're doing the show from a hammock under a tree sipping a fruity drink).

It's always a challenge to find ways to spice up your promotion appearances in the dog days of summer. Remember, after a couple of weeks of summer vacation, kids get bored, parents' patience wears thin and everyone needs a break! Your remotes and appearances can be a great "break" with just a little extra effort. You can be the conduit to make an "ordinary" appearance a tremendous promotional opportunity! Here are a few ideas that may fit your situation:

Rent snow making machines. Take them to any public location and create the **WXXX Snowball Fight**.

Summer ideas and specific 4th of July information is online at tjohnsonmedia.com

Set the tone by having the entire show come in to work wearing bathing suits every Friday. It helps lighten things up and is promotable as **Dog Day Fridays.** When you go to appearances or remotes, invite listeners to do the same. Bring out portable wading pools or a dunk tank!

Take your show live to public pools in your daily **Pool Crawl**. Bring prizes and cool refreshments (soda, ice cream, etc.).

Capture the exhuberance of your younger days, and invite your listeners to a **Sprinkler Party.** Set up a sprinkler and invite listeners to come by to cool off. Serve them lemonade! Simple, inexpensive, *fun.*

Who doesn't love a mid-summer **Water Fight** ? Have your listeners come and have the biggest water fight ever in a public location: Squirt Guns and water balloons are cheap, and you can provide all the tools for a lot of fun!

Your station vehicle for the summer is an **Ice Cream Truck**!!! Paint your call letters all over it, and visit neighborhoods. You can sell the ice cream or give it away. It creates a great reaction, and guarantees instant crowds.

This one hurts. **Best Belly Flop** wins!!!! Set it up at a local pool, one with a pretty decent diving board. Line up a bunch of local celebrity judges (TV anchors, sports figures, etc.) Best and the most painful wins.
Have contestants wear full winter gear and eat hot salsa, hot

links, drink hot tea, hot tamales, and challenge them: **Can You Stand The Heat**? Make sure they hydrate before you do this, and you may want to have a doctor standing by.

Three contestants each have to sit on huge blocks of ice in the studio, wearing just shorts to win **Coolest Seats in the House**. If all last the entire length of the show draw for the winner. All participants get tickets.

Sponsor a softball/volleyball tournament or **Volleyball Marathon**. Try to break the world's record for longest continuous softball or volleyball game. If your market has a sand beach, do it there.

Show us your WXXX at a beach in a **Most Creative Tan** contest.

Media will love covering your **Belly Flop Competition**. Here's some tips to give your participants on making a tidal splash: 1. Jump up and out as far as you can. Put in some practice jumping off the side of the pool before you move on to the diving board. 2. As you rocket forward, extend your arms and legs. Amateurs stay in this position, which is why they scream in pain when they hit the water. 3. Bend your body into the shape of a banana. This will maximize your splashing impact and prevent you from bashing your face or groin. 4. At the last moment, cock your head back to protect your face. For dramatic effect after the splash, bob on the surface like a dead man.

-108-

BACK TO SCHOOL

Most schools start the week before, or the day after, Labor Day. Your sales department will be hounding advertisers for back-to-school sales, and likewise, you should acknowledge this time on the air.

It's appropriate that school should start in September. It's the 9th month, and come Labor Day, mom gets rid of the kids. By the way, parents have learned that a child's greatest period of growth is the month after you buy new school clothes.

Here are some ideas for launching into the season:

Increase word of mouth around local High Schools with a **School Spirit Contest.** High school students are asked to start a petition to get as many signatures as possible to win a concert performance by a current hot artist at their school, hosted by your personalities. Keep the names and phone numbers from the petitions in a data bank for research purposes. Have jocks call periodically to ask about music preferences, what they do for fun, what is happening, etc. There are alternatives to choose the winner:

> ➤ Have them send in postcards, letters.
> ➤ Have them collect aluminum cans or newspapers for

Get more Back to School and Fall promotion ideas online at tjohnsonmedia.com

recycling.

➢ Collect pennies at central locations in their schools. Money collected is donated to charity.

A grocery store chain in your area is likely doing a "save your receipts and win computers for your school" promotion. Try to tie in and promote it in exchange for getting your call letters on all their POP and newspaper ads. Call it **Apples for the Students.**

Get visibility by attending **Pep Rallies and Football Games**.   There is usually a BIG one to start the football season. Give away miniature footballs with the station's logo on it, frisbes, etc.

Give away **limo rides** to school. These can usually be traded out. This can be a feature once a week, and be made available for student use whenever they want to use it.

This is an easy promotion where a student wins a chance to be a **Roadie For A Day** with a hot band coming to town.

Work with record companies to have their artists featured on **Book Covers** with your name and logo. On the back, put your logo, important phone numbers (include your request line). Or, tie in with charity and sell the book covers through student governments.

Tie in with a local sponsor for **Show Us You're A's**. Each time report cards come out, kids come in to "show us your A's" and pick up a small prize. Each A also enters the student for a grand prize drawing at the end of the

Phone topic: Summer romances!

semester for a computer system. This can also turn into a competition between schools. The school with the most A's wins a free dance from the station.

> Go to kindergarten classes with a recorder and talk to kids about their first day of school. When you do, be sure you send home a note to mom and dad telling them that their son or daughter will be on your station the next morning.

> Get a limo and escort kids to school, doing your show live from the limo, then from the school. Make a big deal out of it...keep it focused on K-3rd graders.

> Have listeners call in with memories about their first day in school, first day in a new school, first day in high school, etc.

> Who are the best teachers you ever had? Worst? Why?

> What has changed in the classroom since you were a kid? (Carbon handouts mimeographed instead of copy machines, Glue sticks instead of glue bottles)

> What did your kids have to wear on the first day of school?

THERE'S NO EXCUSE!

Here is a list of actual school excuses from notes sent by parents:

➢ Please excuse John for being absent on January 28,29,30,31,32,33.

➢ Mary couldn't come to school because she was bothered by very close veins.

➢ John has been absent because he had two teeth taken out of his face.

➢ I kept Billie home because she had to go Christmas shopping because I didn't know what size she wears.

➢ Please excuse Gloria. She has been sick under the doctor.

➢ My son is under the doctor's care and should not take P.E. Please execute him.

➢ Susan was absent from school because she had a going over.

➢ Please excuse Robert Monday. He had loose vowels.

➢ Please excuse Blanch from P.E. She feel out of a tree and misplaced her hip.

➢ Please excuse Joyce from Jim (gym). She is administrating.

➢ Carlos was absent because he was playing football. He was hurt in the growing part.

➢ My daughter was absent yesterday because she was tired. She spent the weekend with the Marines.

On Friday mornings, put students on the air talking about how bad their team is going to beat the competition that night.

Junior High

The stress of going into Junior High makes for great radio. A lot of kids are scared to death. The school is bigger, and there are horror stories (some true, but most are "Urban Legends") about being stuffed in a locker or dumpster. Combine that with the hormonal changes taking place, and you have all you need to fill a show for back-to-school week. Take calls from kids (and parents) about these fears.

Rules For Junior High:

> ➢ Who you eat lunch with is more important that what you eat.
> ➢ When posing for a family portrait, make a face.
> ➢ If your parents don't like the music you listen to, turn it up!
> ➢ If it's a really nice day, stay inside and watch TV.
> ➢ If someone of the opposite sex likes you, it is up to your friends whether or not you return the affection.
> ➢ Keep secrets for about 10 minutes.
> ➢ Do not write down phone messages.
> ➢ Look for meaning in bad song lyrics.
> ➢ Ruin things for everyone.
> ➢ Your parents were created to embarrass you... avoid them.

-109-

Labor Day

It's the last weekend of summer, and the time when your audience's mindset shifts. To many, it's a "last blast" of fun before school begins, and to others (parents), it's a relief because the kids are going back to school. At any rate, it's a great chance to promote and market your show and your station.

A great idea for the last week of summer, is to give away tickets to all of your area's biggest and best summer attractions...theme parks, outdoor venues, etc. Promote it as a **Last Gasp Endless Summer**, or a means of extending the summer for a few more weeks! You'll find that the parks are much more enthusiastic about working with you at this time of year, since their volume really slows when the kids go back to school.

Labor Day Weekend has become a popular time for stations to host their annual concert promotions, or station parties. Z100 in Portland has had success with their **Last Chance Summer Dance**. Former Z100 programmer Ken Benson started this event, and it has become a tradition in the city. Book the artists early, and make it fun for the whole family.

Your show gives away, and arranges to deliver fast foods., including pizza, Chinese take-out, etc. to listener's homes or wherever they are gathered. Call it **Labor Day Delivery Blitz.**

The week before Labor Day, arrange to give away a **Day Off With Pay** to winners, so they can extend their weekend into a FOUR day weekend. The grand prize might be an extra WEEK off. After all, we just can't stand the thought of summer ending and going back to work.

While families are out enjoying the last weekend of summer, some of your pregnant listeners will be "celebrating" a much different kind of Labor Day by turning out **Labor Day Babies**. On the day *after,* give away prizes and gifts to parents of babies born on Labor Day.   Have fun with it by offering some twists on the theme: For example, the baby born closest to your station's frequency (if your frequency is 102.7, the baby born at 10:27) would win. You could give away $1,000 in baby prizes to the first woman who goes into labor and calls you from the labor room of hospital (be sure to verify it). Keep her on the phone as long as possible, and talk to the father for some great audio. This is also a good idea to keep for the first baby of the new year!

All those **Summer Movie Blockbusters** that came out around Memorial Day are about to go to video release, in time for Christmas. You could give away copies to all of the summer's hottest movies (including soundtracks) when they become available.

-110-

HALLOWEEN

Different cultures refer to October 31st in different ways: All Saints' Eve, he Eve of Samhain, All Souls' Eve, and All Hallows' Eve, which eventually became Halloween.

The Celts thought Halloween was the time when ghosts returned to roam the Earth. They put on frightening costumes and carved grotesque masks out of gourds to ward off the evil spirits.
 The ancient Romans protected themselves from evil spirits by carving out gourds and placing lit candles inside. Also, in anticipation of visiting (and hungry!) ghosts, they would leave out bread and water.

The ancient Greeks believed that spirits returned once a year to roam the Earth. In order to honor the dead (and keep in their good graces!) they celebrated with a week-long festival. They offered sacrifices to the spirits and performed rituals to ward off the evil spirits.

What about Trick-Or-Treat? There are several different ideas about the origins of trick-or-treating.Some say it began with the Celts who bribed evil people and spirits with treats so they wouldn't be the brunt of tricks and mischief. Those who gave generously would have a good year and

There are hundreds of Halloween ideas for morning shows online at tjohnsonmedia.com

those who didn't were to expect evil spirits to lurk in their lives.

Others say it started with the Druids, Celtic priests, who would ask for food, money, and favors in exchange for saving peoples' souls from evil.

The Irish legend of the Jack-O'-Lantern says that Jack was not allowed to go to heaven after he died because he was a miser. Neither was he allowed to go to hell because he played practical jokes on the devil. So he was forced to walk the Earth, carrying only his lantern, until Judgement day.

Samhain was considered The Lord of Death by the Celts and they held festivals every year in order to ward off his evil. It was said that he reincarnated the souls of evil people into black cats. Now you know why people are superstitious of black cats, and with good reason, according to the Celts!

Do you know the origin of saying "God bless you" after someone sneezes? It was thought by the Welsh that if you sneezed on Halloween your soul escaped for an instant and if someone didn't bless you, the devil would steal it away!

There is a Scottish superstition that says every Halloween the devil appears somewhere in the country wearing a kilt and playing a ghostly tune on the bagpipes!

Anoka, Minnesota is "The Halloween Capital of the World!" Every year there is a weeklong festival that almost every town member participates in. There are activities for all ages, parties, contests, and parades.

Today, Halloween is celebrated mostly in English-speaking countries such as Ireland, Canada, and, of course, the United States.

> **About Witches:** On the night of a full moon members of the Old Religion danced around a bonfire astride broomsticks and harvest tools. "Witches" performed this ritual in anticipation of a rich harvest!

Get out those camcorders and tape recorders. Jerking around with those trick or treaters makes for great audio the next morning.

-111-

HALLOWEEN IDEAS

Send out **"Halloween Safety Packets"** to area schools, consisting of reflective safety strips, trick-or-treat bags and reflective stickers. Print your logo on the bags.

Dress up as vampires and solicit donors for your **Blood Drive** at a local blood bank. Give away special prizes for donors.

Pumpkins are becoming more and more creative every year. Have a **Show us your Pumpkin** contest, including a prize for the most creative use of a pumpkin involving use of your station's call letters.

Designate ___ houses in your area as a secret WXXX **Mystery Monster Cash** house. The first person to knock on that person's door and say WXXX...Trick or Treat wins the cash. This gets a LOT of people saying your calls all over town. You can also put a mystery man or woman at various Halloween parties around town, and the first person to say WXXX Trick or Treat to that person wins the cash.

Organize a **Nightmare on Elm Street** Film Festival with all 5 "Freddie" movies. Listeners dressed as Freddie get in free.

Throw your city's biggest Halloween Party at a listener's home for the **Nightmare on YOUR Street**. Bring all the food, drinks, sound system, etc. and have your jocks host it. You could call it a "Nightmare on YOUR street". For a real exclamation point on this promotion, have an artist or two show up. Give away something that listeners can't buy at any price! Be sure to have contests, games, music, and of course the costume contest!

Have your morning show broadcast **Live From the Haunted House.** It can be a real, local house, or do it with theater of the mind and broadcast from a fictitious haunted house. Use sfx, echo, etc. to create a full audio atmosphere. This should be set up and teased a few days in advance with listeners calling in to tell you all about this haunted house they know about, etc. Better yet, find a local house reputed to be haunted, and do the show from there!

Broadcast from a public location the day after Halloween, soliciting **Trick Or Treat Leftovers,** leftover candy that wasn't given away. Give it to a children's home.

Too Much Candy is bad for you, of course…but how MUCH candy is *too* much? Bring in three kids on the day after Halloween…fill them up with Snickers bars and other candy to see how much candy causes the first one to get sick!

The Great Pumpkin Olympics are always a lot of fun. You can do it in three simple steps: 1. Find a central place to have the Olympics. Make sure the place you pick will allow pumpkin guts to spill all over their lot.　2. Get about three dozen pumpkins.　3. Invite listeners to come by on their way to work to play games like pumpkin bowling, the pumpkin-put (like the shot put), pumpkin toss for distance. pumpkin seed spitting contest, pumpkin pie eating contest, pumpkin smashing (of course).

HALLOWEEN PHONE TOPICS

➤ What Is Your Favorite Halloween Candy?
➤ Have you ever had a ghost encounter?
➤ Is your house haunted?
➤ When are you too old to trick or treat?
➤ What's the scariest movie of all time?
➤ Ever seen a UFO?
➤ What kind of candy are you giving out this year?
➤ What is your favorite kind of candy from when you went trick or treating?
➤ Have you ever gone through your kid's bags and taken the "good stuff"?
➤ What local celebrity needs no costume for Halloween?
➤ Most frightening local Halloween display?
➤ What is the most scared you've ever been?
➤ Pranks that worked, pranks that didn't?
➤ What is your Ouija board story?
➤ What are local celebrities giving out for Trick or Treat?
➤ Do as many kids come to your door as they used to?
➤ What is the lamest thing people ever gave you/ your kids?

-112-

SOUND EFFECTS THEATER

This is a good bit anytime. You get a listener on the phone to provide the sound effects while you tell the story. Every time you pause, that's their cue to react.

Here's a story for Halloween:

One Halloween night, I walked down a lonesome road and I could hear the wind howling (sfx). As I walked past the local cat meowed menacingly and ran across my path (sfx)! To avoid having the cat cross my path, I walked through the back yard of a large, spooky-looking house. I stopped when I thought I heard someone faintly crying for help inside (sfx). I moved closer to a window and the cry for help got louder (sfx). Suddenly, I heard a blood curdling scream (sfx)! And the laugh of a homicidal maniac (sfx). And then I heard what sounded like ghosts (sfx). Startled, I ran around to the front of the house and accidentally stepped on the black cat (sfx)! I froze in terror as all the sounds from inside the house stopped and the front door slowly creaked open (sfx). Then it slowly creaked shut (sfx). Then I heard footsteps on the porch coming towards me (sfx) and wolves began howling in the distance (sfx). Even though I was frightened out of my mind, I stood still as a Dominoes Pizza delivery man walked up to me and handed me a large pizza. This was no ordinary pizza delivery man, as he wore a black cape over his uniform & he gave a spooky laugh as held out his hand for the money (sfx). I handed him a fifty dollar bill and he stood staring menacingly at me as a lone wolf howled in the distance (sfx). Suddenly he flung his cape and hissed "Fool! You know I don't carry that much change! Now you will die!" And he laughed hysterically as he showed his vampire fangs (sfx)! I grabbed my fifty and began running with the pizza as fast as I could! All I could hear was my heavy breathing (sfx) and the vampire delivery man behind me revving the engine of his Dominoes delivery car, a shiny black Ford. Entering a cemetery, I whistled a tune to ease my nerves (sfx). I could hear an owl somewhere in the distance (sfx). Suddenly, a black Fiesta (sfx)! But luck was with me! The vampire delivery man ran a stop sign and was pulled over by the cops. Very much relieved, I walked home, grabbed a soda from the fridge and sat down on the couch to eat my pizza. But when I opened the pizza, I froze with fear as I looked upon the most horrific sight any pizza lover could behold! I screamed in terror as I looked upon a large pizza... with anchovies! (sfx)

From The Desk Of...Peggy Noonan.

"TV gives everyone an image, but radio gives birth to a million images in a million brains."

Peggy Noonan is an author and presidential speechwriter

-113-

THANKSGIVING

This is one of those holidays that is difficult to promote around. It's a sentimental, family holiday, and is the gateway to the grand-daddy of all holidays, Christmas!

When putting together any promotional plans, you should consider very carefully:

1. Your station's essence: If you are a more conservative station that targets upper demos, then "Turkey Bowling" is not for you.

2. Balance. Don't treat sentimental holidays with total irreverence. If you are outrageous with some promotional elements, offset that with something like a "Food Drive for the Needy".

Above all, go the extra mile and make your promotional plans SPECIAL. Cut through the hype and clutter and make it an event that causes people to talk about your station! Here are a few ideas for you:

Don't forget to resurrect Adam Sandler's classic, "The Turkey Song"

Have volunteers sit in a tub of cranberry sauce for a day to win a vacation to the islands or cash in the **Cranberry Vacation for Two**.

More for Thanksgiving is available online at tjohnsonmedia.com

One of the highlights of the day is Macy's Parade. You could create an "on-air" **Thanksgiving Parade** which will air the day before Turkey Day. Incorporate air-staff as correspondents along the parade route, talk about the floats, produce the bands marching up and away from the microphones.

Thanksgiving weekend is a time when everyone overeats, so promote it with **Stuff Yourself!**! Solicit up to 10 contestants on Wednesday, and have a weigh-in live on the air. Their instructions are to see who can gain the most weight by Monday morning, when you hold another weigh-in and award prizes.

A great way to trigger contests over Thanksgiving week is to give away prizes to people who can have **Fun With Mom or Grandma**. Get their MOTHER or GRANDMOTHER on the air to "gobble" for their turkeys.

Your caller has 10-seconds to **Beat the Turkey Timer**! They name 5-Thanksgiving themes in a category. Then after 10-seconds, the turkey timer pops up. It sounds like a tweeking/blowing noise, made with your mouth. Pretty cornball, but it works!

Hold this at a club Thanksgiving weekend: **The Butterball Belly Contest**. Contestants rub butter on their bellies, line up and compete in various categories...Best Belly, Biggest Belly, Beer Belly, etc. etc. Winners get turkeys, short term memberships to health clubs, free liposuction, etc.

Get a junk car donated by a car dealer and drive around your **Turkey Mobile** with the driver dressed in a turkey outfit. Hand out free turkey dinners and register to win the car.

Use frozen turkeys as bowling balls down the aisle of grocery stores and take your listeners **Turkey Bowling**.

Turkeys dropped from helicopters? The **Turkey Drop** is a promotion in honor of fictitious newsman Les Nessman. You REALLY drop certificates for a free turkey attached to paper Hallmark Turkeys. Do it for a large crowd.

Remember that more people are using the long weekend as a mini-vacation, and are avoiding the normal family sit-down. Thanksgiving is the busiest day of the year at airports.

From the Desk of...Arthur Carlson

"With God as my witness, I thought turkeys could fly."

‑Arthur Carlson, GM of fictional radio station WKRP in Cincinnati!

-114-

ON A SERIOUS NOTE...

Your show and listeners record serious, sincere Thanksgiving messages. Play over intros in place of sweepers or as "montage" promos. Or, you can make it into a "What I'm Thankful For" message.

Thanksgiving Food Drive

Work with clients to organize drop off points for food. You might even broadcast live from some of the drop points Thanksgiving week. Be sure you have your banners up in full view. You could even use the "Mayflower" idea and launch your campaign to fill an entire Mayflower truck with food for the poor. Try to tie in with a large public location (major grocery store or chain?) to park your truck. If you can stage a stunt, you will get more attention (roof sit?) This encourages shoppers to pick up some extra food while shopping, and gets your call letters in front of new cume.

Coats for Cold

This is the perfect time to launch a "Coats for the Cold" campaign or one that collects food and clothing for the needy. Important: It's vital that you focus your promotional attention on a tangible, personal organization that will receive the donated items. Make it as clearly focused and "one to one" as possible. Try to eliminate the "middleman" in promoting the event. Focus on "Everything we collect is going directly into the hands of people who have had a tough year and could use a sack of groceries or clothes...(organization) is helping us with distribution." The point is, don't let the collected items disappear into a "black hole" charity that listeners can't relate to. Also, focus on what you are going to collect and who it is going to benefit. Don't try to collect "anything" for the "needy". Pinpoint that you are going for blankets for the cold or food for the hungry. You'll have much better response if you tell listeners exactly *what* you want them to do.

It's a Fact!

➢ The Turkey Capital of the World is Rockingham County, Va. They are loaded with turkey farms .

➢ Turkeys are very dumb....if you shake a stick in front of a turkey, it will have a heart attack and die...if you put an empty five gallon drum in a pen full of turkeys, they will jump in the drum until it is full of turkeys and all will smother.

➢ An average slice of pumpkin pie contains 180 calories and six grams of fat. A slice of cherry pie has 350 calories and 16 grams of fat. Apple pie has 410 calories and 22 grams of fat...Pecan pie? 412 calories, 19 grams of fat.

-115-

Dinner on the Mayflower

This is an old promotion, and is very effective the first time it's done in a market, or if your station is the one who's done it in the past. If someone else has done it in prior years, stay away from it. Anyway, here's a checklist of "to do's":

A) Get Mayflower moving van!

B) Clean up the van. Paint inside walls white if possible.

C) Get prestigious local restaurant to cater with all the fancy dishware, napkins... formal dinner style!

D) If possible, get temporary chandalier or candles for the table setting!

E) Go to the local college and get a four-piece string quartet. They'll probably do it for practice, fun and publicity for the college.

F) Dress up at least 4 of your on air personalities in tuxes and have them wait on the winning family personally. This little touch is the key to the whole promotion! It's the personal touch from you!

G) Solicit winners by having listeners use a point of purchase to register... or simply send in a postcard.

H) On T-Day, drive the Mayflower Van to the winner's home and park in front of the house! Or, find the highest profile location in your city and Ta-da... "Dinner on the Mayflower!"

Benjamin Franklin called the bald eagle "a bird of bad moral character" because of its hunting habits. His unpopular choice for our national bird was, of course, the turkey.

-116-

THE DAY AFTER

➢ LEFTOVERS: Starting the day after Thanksgiving, listen for the sound of the refrigerator door. The ___th caller wins turkey sandwiches (leftovers) from local sandwich shop or deli, along with leftover prizes that winners forgot to claim. Or, they call in and trade leftover turkey for other prizes (T-shirts, albums, etc). By the way, the Leftover Hotline is 800-972-2784.

➢ Give away health club memberships to help get rid of all that weight you put on at Thanksgiving.

➢ The Day AFTER Thanksgiving (and the following Saturday too) are the busiest shopping days of the year. Consider having your station's logo produced on shopping bags, then hand them out in malls as people enter. Great visibility. Broadcast live from the malls if appropriate.

➢ Also, consider doing your morning show live from a mall at an area you arrange to have free childcare while parents take advantage of early sales.

-117-

KINDERGARTEN KITCHEN!

Ask listeners to have their kids describe how to cook a Thanksgiving Turkey. Their descriptions make great material. Here are some examples: (spelling is verbatim)

➢ By the turkey take the wrapper off. Den I will cok it and I will tak it out. I will eet it... mee and my feelee.

➢ Put sale on your big tukey... put stofing in it... put it in oven for ten hours.

➢ By the turkey... thaw the turkey. Put turkey in oven for 3 hours at 550 degrees. Take burnt turkey out of oven, throw it away, and go to McDonalds.

➢ Go to Piggly Wiggly and get a turkey. Then shoot it. Then pluck the feathers off. Smuther choclate all over. Stick in oven cook it for an hour. Take it out, put a bomb in it, put more choclate eat it expload into peaces and surprise... you throw up!

➢ You put a spel on your freiend and turn him into a turkey and drop an anvil on him. Put in oven with two thousand matches. For toppings, put some syrup, pepperoni, appleasause, itching powder, cat guts, suntan lotion, sand, and vomit. Eat some more. (hey, they wrote them, I didn't)

➤ First by the turkey, then cut the inside put it in oven for one hour. Then take it out, put a lot of oil, like 25 gallons. Put it in oven for 25 minutes. Then get out and eat it.

➤ Kill a turkey. Bye bye you stupid turkey! Pluck it bok bok bogok. Cook it there's your dinner!

-118-

CHRISTMAS

Although Christmas is traditionally celebrated on December 25th, the precise date on which Jesus of Nazareth was born is a matter of some debate. Although it marks the start of the modern calendar, even the year of Jesus' birth is uncertain. Since the birth occurred during the reign of King Herod, scholars calculate that Jesus must have been born between four and eight years B.C. - that is, in the era that is commonly called "Before Christ." Apparently, the man who in 534 A.D. first calculated the year of Jesus' birth was not a mathematician.

One reason for this uncertainty is that the stories of his birth, recorded in the New Testament books of Matthew and Luke, were written several decades after the event. And those who wrote of it gave no specific dates for the event.

Today Christmas is more than a one-day celebration, or a 12-day festival. It is part of a lengthy holiday season embracing at least the whole month of December. In the United States the holiday season begins on Thanksgiving Day and ends on January 1.

The reason for this extended holiday period is that Christmas is no longer only a religious festival. It is also the most popular holiday period for everyone in countries

There are more Christmas ideas than you can use, online at tjohnsonmedia.com

where Christianity has become the dominant religion. Even in Japan, where Christianity is in the minority, Christmas has become a festive, gift-giving holiday time.

 Mistletoe is a parasite that grows on fir trees. The druids, a Celtic religious order of priests and soothsayers, thought it was a symbol of peace for a bird called the mistle thrush to carry the plant in it's claws. They believed a sprig of mistle thrush toe, or mistletoe, could make warriors drop their weapons and hug each other. The kissing custom evolved from that.

If you hang a stocking on Christmas Eve, thank St. Nicholas. A 4th century figure and another early form of Santa Claus, St. Nick provided for the three daughters of a nobleman, placing gold by their beds for their wedding dowries. One night, however, he slipped, and gold fell in a stocking hung up to dry.

-119-

SANTA CLAUS

Who is Santa Claus? Is he only a fairy tale? A farce? If so, why do we give him so many names (Old Saint Nick, Father Christmas, Kris Kringle, The Jolly Old Man in the Red Suit, etc) Why do we wait in lines for hours so our children can sit on his lap? Or stand in the freezing cold so that we can wave to him as he passes by on a float in the Macy's Parade? If Santa Claus merely is a myth, why do we spend so much of our time and creative energy to convince our children he is real? Is it a lie?

The Santa Claus tradition has not survived for centuries simply to keep the Hallmarks and the Macy's and the gift wrapping manufacturers of this world in business. No, there is a method behind this madness. Santa Claus serves as a reminder of the pleasure of giving without thank-yous, of a child's unyeilding imagination, the power of believing in things that are impossibly good, and the willingness to believe that if we are good, good things will happen. Santa Clause could not possibly be a lie.
Perhaps Santa Claus was best described over 100 years ago by late Frank P. Church, in an editorial in the New York Sun, Sept. 21, 1897.

"Yes, Virginia, there is a SANTA CLAUS. He exists as

certainly as love and generosity and devotion exist, and you know that they abound and give to your life its highest beauty and joy. Alas! how dreary would be the world if there were no SANTA CLAUS! It would be as dreary as if there were no Virginias. There would be no child-like faith then, no poetry, no romance to make tolerable this existence. We should have no enjoyment, except in sense and sight. The eternal light with which childhood fills the world would be extinguished."

-120-

SANTA FACTS

There are 2 billion children (persons under 18) in the world. But since Santa doesn't appear to handle Muslim, Hindu, Jewish and Buddhist children, that reduces the workload to 15% of the total-378 million according to Population Reference Bureau. At an average rate of 3.5 children per household, that's 91.8 million homes. One presumes there to be at least one good child in each.

Santa has 31 hours of Christmas to work with, due to the different time zones and the rotation of the earth, assuming he travels east to west (which seems logical). This works out to 822.6 visits per second. This is to say that for each Christian household with good children, Santa has1/1000th of a second to park, hop out of the sleigh, jump down the chimney, fill the stockings, distribute the remaining presents under the tree, eat whatever snacks have been left out, get back up the chimney, get back to the sleigh and move onto the next house. Assuming that each of these 91.8 million stops are evenly distributed around the earth (which, of course, we know to be false but for the purposes of our calculations we will accept). We are now talking about 78 miles per household, a total trip of 75-1/2 million miles, not counting stops to do what most of us must do at least once every 31 hours, plus feeding and etc. This means Santa's sleigh is moving at 650 miles per second, 3,000 times the speed of sound. For purposes of comparisons, the fastest man-made vehicle on Earth, the Ulysses space probe, moves at a poky 27.4 miles per second-a conventional reindeer can run, tops, 15 miles per hour.

The payload on the sleigh adds another interesting element. Assuming that each child gets nothing more than a medium sized lego set (2 pounds) the sleigh is carrying 321,300 tons, not counting Santa, who invariably is described as overweight. On land, conventional reindeer can pull no more than 300 pounds. Even granting that "flying reindeer" could pull ten times the normal amount, we cannot do the job with eight or even nine. We need 214,200 reindeer. This increases the payload-not even counting the weight of the sleigh-to 353,430 tons.

353,000 tons traveling at 650 miles per second creates enormous air resistance-this will heat the reindeer up in the same fashion as spacecrafts re-entering the earths atmosphere. The lead pair of reindeer will absorb 14.3 quintillion joules of energy per second each. In short, they will burst into flames almost instantaneously, exposing the reindeer behind them, and create deafening sonic booms in their wake. The entire reindeer team will be vaporized within 4.26 thousandths of a second. Santa, meanwhile, will be subjected to centrifugal forces 17,500.06 times greater than gravity. A 250 pound Santa (which seems ludicrously slim) would be pinned to the back of his sleigh by 4,315,015 pounds of force.

In conclusion: If Santa ever did deliver presents on Christmas Eve, he's dead now.

You might want to do this bit when you are sure the kids have gone off to school. You're sure to infuriate some parents when their children hear their favorite morning show announce that Santa is a fairy tale!

-121-

How to Sound Like Christmas

This is the busiest time of the year. Lifestyles are altered, everyone is hustling about and personal schedules take on a new look. YOUR schedule changes as well, and the pace becomes more frantic.

It is more important than ever to stay focused on the product of your radio station. With more people shopping at night and on weekends, you have a unique opportunity to attract new cume and more quarter hours to your station.

Pay special attention to all programming elements. Is the music well mixed to represent your position each quarter hour? Are you properly promoting that position through liners, sweepers and promos? With the increased spot load this time of year, are other non-music elements under control? Are the personalities on the air RELATING to the audience and the activities that are important to the target?

With lifestyles changing, what better time to capture and convert new listeners? Your competitors are not paying as close attention to their station as you will be to yours. Turn it into an advantage to score big gains.

Playing Christmas songs is not the only way to "sound like Christmas" to your listeners. Here are some suggestions:

Recut some of your sweepers using some holiday sound effects (Sleigh bells, Santa's HO HO HO, a subtle hook of a familiar traditional Christmas song, etc).

Have special holiday jingles cut using your present package. Most jingle companies offer this service at a reasonable fee.

On station promos, be careful not to *overuse* Christmas
music beds. So many clients will be running spots with holiday
backgrounds that your promo could be lost in the shuffle.

Use audio drops from Christmas movies, familiar specials, comedy albums, etc. A great way to use these is over an instrumental bed leading up to a jingle.

Record children (elementary schools would be glad to cooperate) wishing listeners a Merry Christmas from themselves and your station. Also play some asking Santa for gifts, with a mention of your calls of course.

The important thing is to be PERCEIVED as the Christmas Station.

-122-

CHRISTMAS IDEAS

Your station is probably planning a major promotion around the Holiday season, so this section focuses more on what you can do in your show leading up to the world's most observed holiday!

If your station is NOT involved in any charitable angle, step in to help needy organizations such as: Toys For Tots, Food For the Homeless, etc. You might tie in with local TV stations for added media power and exposure, but don't let them get all the credit for the promotion. A great angle for this is the SHARING SLEIGH.

You could also check with your local transportation company and see about a joint venture for **Stuff A Bus**. You borrow a bus for a couple of weeks, take out the seats, etc. and drive around to different locations for listeners to come and fill it up with toys, clothing, food, etc.

Dress up as **Santa Claus**, walk up to people in the mall and pay for their purchases, compliments of WXXX's SECRET SANTA. This is similar to the Mystery Man stunt described earlier.

If you live in a military community, contact your armed forces organization and see if you can arrange to send messages to loved ones that can't be home for the holidays. You could dedicate your Christmas Eve programming to having their relatives on your station sending messages, etc.

Get a listener on the line and call a local convenience store to play the **FA-LA-LA-LA-LA Game**. When they answer the phone, the listener says "Deck the Halls With Boughs of Holly" and then of course to win the clerk must say Fa-La-La-La-La-La-La-La-La."

Go to local elementary schools and record children saying "Merry Christmas" or their own personal **Holiday Greetings**. Send home a note for mom and dad, telling them to be listening to your station to hear their child on the air. Edit and produce the messages into 15-20 second promos and run frequently!

Set A World Record for reading "Twas The Night Before Christmas". As of this writing, it is 49 seconds. So, take calls all morning trying to beat it.

Fax the words to a Christmas Carol to an office and solicit listeners to be part of your **Office Christmas Karaoke**. Have them do the tune on the air.

Record the audio of the top selling toys of the year. Listeners call in to try and identify the toy when you play it. If they name it, they win the toy for playing **Noise Toys**.

Listeners call in to ask where to find a gift they are looking for, and others call to tell them where to get it in WXXX **Gift Information Exchange**.

Set up an answering machine and invite listeners to call in with their personal **Christmas Messages** to someone they love. Play them back the week before Christmas. Use the best tapes, of course. It's not necessary, but you could also offer a small prize for listeners hearing a message to them.

Have women who want to find out what their husbands are buying them for Christmas call in to **Sneak A Peek**. Then call husbands and pose as callers from Consumer Research asking men about their Christmas gift selections. Wife is on the line too, and tells jock what to suggest or what to return.

Let (x) number of dads all try to build the same bike (out of the box) in the Christmas version of **Some Assembly Required**. Dad who can assemble the quickest, with all the parts, wins.

Stand one of your flunkies up in the corner at a business and let listeners bring in lights, ornaments, etc., to decorate him as a
Human Christmas Tree.

Listeners fax in their name, address and phone number if they have tacky, cheesy Christmas light demonstrations. You put it all together and organize the **Tacky Christmas Tour**. Post the route on your web site and arrange a tour of the most obnoxious.

Your show goes **Christmas Shopping** for a listener. Get the sad stories about how listeners hate to shop. Pick a winner and go buy the items on their list.

Instead of giving away fruitcakes, have listeners bring those unwanted fruitcakes to the station and **Toss The Fruit Cake**. Award prizes for accuracy, distance, biggest "splat".

Get all the favorite Christmas movies together, arrange a theater and hold a **Christmas Movie Film Festival** for a Saturday full of free Christmas Movies.

Start a **Christmas Tree Price War** the last week of Christmas among stands that will offer the lowest prices. Start at $30 and go lower from there...they have to keep the trees at the low price until noon.

Splice together the word SANTA from every Christmas Song you can find. Put together a 4-5 song Santa Montage, and you have an instant contest called **Name That Santa.**

Letters To Santa is always a winner. Set up a post office box and have letters sent that you can use on the air, or set up a voice mail and have kids leave messages for Santa. Here are some actual letters:

> ➤ Dear Santa, Please don't leave me any toys that cost less than ten dollars. Last year you only left me cheap toys. Love, Bryan.
> ➤ Dear Santa, I want a baseball bat that can hit home runs. The bat I got last year strikes out too much. Your Friend, Willy.
> ➤ Dear Santa, Last Christmas you left me a sled. This Christmas please leave some snow. Your pal, Jed.

> Dear Santa, How much do you make? Do you make more than the president? I hope so because you make more people happy than the president. Jane.

Christmas Postmarks

All you have to do is address and stamp all your cards, place them in a big envelope, and mail them to one of the following addresses:
> Post Office, North Pole, Alaska, 99705
> Post Office, Santa Claus, Indiana, 47579
> Post Office, Snowflake, Arizona, 85937
> Post Office, Bethlehem, Pennsylvania, 18015
> Post Office, Christmas, Florida, 32709

Get a Santa outfit and offer your listeners **Pictures With Santa** at any retail store. (how about photos with Santa in bed.) Or just take a bed to your appearances and do the same.

Print station **Wrapping Paper**, or station Christmas ornaments. Hire people to wrap gifts for free!

Another emotional winner is **Home for the Holidays**. You can send someone to their home for the holidays, expenses paid. Or, bring someone to your home for the holidays. Solicit entries with who, what, why, etc. via letter or answering
machine. Each day for a couple of weeks (if possible), give away the prize. Sentimental, emotional and perfect for the season.

A good hook for your giveaways is the **12 Days of Christmas.**

Give away prizes each of the 12 days leading up to Christmas. Increase the value of the prizes each day. This promotion is easy to tie into sponsors and clients. Another option is to acquire prizes that are impossible to get. For example, items belonging to celebrities (Janet Jackson's swimsuit, etc). Then everyone who wins one of these prizes qualifies for a grand prize.

Take charge and generate community pride by providing a **Giant Christmas Tree** in a highly visible location, making it the public's focal point. Put call letters on the site, but don't over-commercialize it. Invite listeners to come by and donate for charities (Salvation Army, Food Pantries, Homeless Shelters, Toys For Tots, Mitten/coat drives, etc.). Have a huge lighting ceremony, with plenty of live broadcasts throughout the season.

-123-

CHRISTMAS WISH

Without question, this is the best promotion for the Holiday Season, and one of the best promotions PERIOD. Listeners are asked to enter a child, individual or family that has a need at Christmas. The person CAN be themself, but is much more effective if listeners nominate others.

The concept is "If a family member, friend or you are down and out...maybe you can't afford a tree, toys for your kids, a nice Christmas dinner, you're having trouble paying the electric bill...send a letter with your Christmas Wish. Include your name, address, day/night phone number and the information about the person you are writing in for. We promise to read all letters we receive, and we'll grant a many wishes as we can to make this your best Christmas possible."

Each day in December, the radio station selects a letter and provides for that Christmas Wish to be met. The more needy, more emotional, the better.Be sure to start soliciting early in the season (Mid-November), especially if you have never done the promotion before.

On air execution is simple. Each day, one of the jocks (same one) should read the entry, call the person submitting

the wish, and grant the wish. Play back the wish all day
long until the next day's wish is granted. This promotion is
extremely sentimental, emotional, entertaining and a
WINNER!

You'll need 2-3 people to read the letters, weed out the
"greed factor" and get on the phones to try and find vendors
to help with the wishes. Most of your advertisers will want
to help you out.

-124-

CHRISTMAS POP QUIZ

- ➤ In the television special "Rudolph The Red Nosed Reindeer" she was Rudolph's girlfriend. Clarice.
- ➤ In the Christmas carol "We Wish You A Merry Christmas" the guests demand that the host bring "this" right now or right here. Figgie pudding.
- ➤ In the poem "Twas the night before Christmas" Santa rose up the chimney after doing this with his finger. "Laying a finger aside of his nose
- ➤ It was this that brought Frosty the Snowman to life. Magic hat
- ➤ This former monster reads "How the Grinch Stole Christmas". Boris Karloff
- ➤ He is the director of the Christmas pageant in a "Charlie Brown Christmas." Charlie Brown.
- ➤ In this carol the lyrics sing "Christmas is coming, the goose is getting fat." The next line suggests that you please put one of these in one of these. "A penny" in the "old man's hat".
- ➤ Of this incomplete list of Santa's reindeer: Donner, Cupid, Dasher, Blitzen, Comet, Rudolph, Dancer, Vixen... this one is omitted. Dancer.
- ➤ It is the government agency that verified Santa Claus' identity in the movie "Miracle on 34th Street." Post Office.
- ➤ In the "Twelve Days of Christmas" if each day only

the first type of gift was given, how many gifts would it total? 78.

➢ This is where "There arose such a clatter." "On the lawn".

➢ Jim Backus and Morey Amsterdam provided the voices for what animated version of a Dickens classic? "Mr. Magoo's Christmas Carol".

➢ In "Up On A House Top," what does Nell want from Santa? A dolly that laughs and cries.

➢ What evergreen tree is considered the least desirable Christmas tree? The spruce.

➢ What is the name of Scrooge's clerk? Bob Cratchit.

➢ What was the biggest selling Christmas item in 1957? The Hula Hoop.

➢ What was the first name of Scrooge's dead partner, Marley? Jacob.

➢ In "It's a Wonderful Life" what was George Bailey's brother's name? Harry.

➢ Frosty the Snowman had coals for eyes and a corn-cob pipe. What did the kids use to make his nose? A button.

➢ How did Frosty come alive? When they put a silk top hat on his head.

➢ What is the original title of the poem, "'Twas The Night Before Christmas?" "A Visit With Saint Nicholas."

➢ What's the name of the Grinch's dog from "The Grinch Who Stole Christmas?" Max.

➢ How long does the average kid spend in Santa's lap at Macy's Department Store? Just 37 seconds.

-125-

CHRISTMAS PHONE BITS

- Who is the biggest grinch you know?
- How do your pets react to your Christmas tree?
- Are you supposed to buy gifts for the mail carrier, trash man, etc? What is the proper etiquette and why?
- Obnoxious relatives you are not looking forward to seeing for the holidays, and why
- Finish this sentence: "It's not Christmas until..."
- What does your kid want for Christmas that they definitely WON'T get.
- What do you eat at Christmas that people think is weird?
- Why do men wait until the last minute to go Christmas shopping?
- Where is the best place to look at Christmas lights?
- Where is the TACKIEST decorated house in town?
- How did you find out that there is no Santa Claus?
- What is the most unusual or strange Christmas tradition that you celebrate at your home?
- Office Party Horror Stories. The one who calls in the best stories wins a fabulous prize selected especially for them.
- What do you say when you get a stupid present?
- What relative could you do without during the holidays?
- What's the coolest thing you have on your Christmas

tree?

- When do you put up your tree?
- Do you leave a snack for Santa on Christmas Eve? If so what?
- When and how do you open your gifts?
- Presents you hate to get!
- What's the stupidest gift you ever returned?
- Have you ever been returning a gift, and then run into the person who gave it to you (while you were returning it)?
- Do you hang up stockings for your pets?
- Whats the lamest gift you ever got for Christmas, and from whom?
- [Fill in the Blank] "Dear Santa. What ever you do this year, please do not leave me _____."
- Where is the Cheapest Christmas Tree?
- 64% of adults can not remember what their spouse gave them for Christmas last year. Line up callers who don't know what you're going to ask them. Then, see if they can tell you what they got.
- Stupidest gifts received?
- Once you discovered there is no Santa, did you snoop for your presents as a kid (or even now)?
- Did you ever open a Christmas present early without your parents knowing about it?"
- What is in your refrigerator that is left over from Thanksgiving?
- Company Christmas Party Horror Stories?
- Does your husband buy good (but not expensive) gifts? How do you get him to step it up?
- Where do you hide Christmas presents?
- What gag gifts do you exchange at Christmas?

PART 8: SHOW PREP
THOUGHT-STARTERS FOR EACH MONTH

-126-

JANUARY

It's a whole new year and a great time for your morning show to launch a fresh, new approach. It's really a pretty easy month for radio. You have the Christmas holiday wrap-up, New Year's resolutions, the Super Bowl and more!

➤ March Of Dimes Birth Defect Prevention Month
➤ National Fiber Month
➤ Soup Month
➤ National Cosmotology Month. Get someone from a cosmetology school to teach makeup tips to your listeners where they need it...in a car during rush hour.
➤ National Diet Month
➤ National Oatmeal Month.
➤ National Prune Breakfast Month. Isn't that convenient?
➤ The best month of the year for sales at department stores.
➤ The first week of January is Universal Letter Writing Week. Send a letter to strange people and wait for their response. Have listeners help you compose it.

You know it's January when...
➤ The stores offer 95% off Christmas merchandise.
➤ The warm holiday feelings are completely gone. Everybody in the family hates each other again.

- ➤ The envelopes with the little windows are coming every day now.
- ➤ The colors of Red and Green make you sick.
- ➤ H&R Block starts advertising.
- ➤ The stupid people that won the Publisher's Clearing House giveaway show up on the TV every ten minutes.
- ➤ The only holiday cookies left over are green ones with jelly inside.

If this is an presidential election year, the inaugural celebration is this month. Obviously, you could send listeners to the gala. In any event, be sure to have tape rolling to capture the events for on air use.

New Year's Eve/Day and Super Bowl ideas are in the section on Holidays in this book

Shedding Holiday Pounds

L osing weight, or getting in shape, is always the #1 New Year's Resolution. Here's some material you can modify to fit your show and relate to those listeners!

Rules For Dieting!

1. If you eat something and no one sees you eat it, it has no calories.

2. If you drink a diet soda with a candy bar, the calories in the candy are cancelled by the diet drink.

3. When you eat with someone else, calories don't count if you don't eat more than they do.

4. Food used for medicinal purposes never count, such as hot chocolate, brandy or other spirits.

5. If you fatten up everyone else around you, then you look thinner.

6. Movie related foods do not have additional calories because they are part of the entire entertainment package.

7. Cookie pieces contain no calories. The process of breaking causes calorie leakage.

8. Foods licked off knives and spoons have no calories if you are in the process of preparing something.

9. Foods that have the same color have the same number of calories. For example, spinach and pistachio ice cream; mushrooms and white chocolate.

10. Chocolate is the universal food coloring and may be substituted for any other food color.

MEN ARE FROM MARS....THE WINTER COLD VERSION!

Why is it that men can go thru severe accidents, air raids, and any other major crisis but always seem to think they're at deaths door when they have a cold? Here' what women and men say when they're not feeling well:

She says:

➢ My nose is a little runny.
➢ I have a sore throat.
➢ I'm a little achy. I wonder if I'm catching that flu going around. I hope this antibiotic kicks in soon.

He says:

➢ I'm allergic to my job.
➢ Do I still have tonsils?
➢ Do you have the phone number for the ambulance?
➢ Do I have disability insurance?

-127-

FEBRUARY

February is a nasty weather month in most cities. Other than Valentine's Day, not much is happening. It's cold, dark, dreary and listeners get cabin fever. It is the month most likely to produce weather induced school closings.

On the other hand, it's also one of the most popular months for ski trips and winter FUN. So, instead of complaining all month long, celebrate **National Blah Buster Month.** The idea is to
provide comfort to all who suffer the Winter Blahs, and remind people that Spring is just around the corner. You can give away ski trips or send listeners to warm weather locations such as Bahamas, Bermuda, Florida, California or Mexico. Better yet, organize a getaway and go along! Or, go cheap and give away tanning salon certificates!

- ➢ American Heart Month
- ➢ Snack Food Month
- ➢ Canned Food Month
- ➢ Pancake Week is sometime this month
- ➢ French Fry Friday is EVERY Friday in February
- ➢ Creative Romance Month designed to keep the sizzle in their relationship by celebrating romance in unique

Valentine's Day ideas are in the section on Holidays in this book

ways.
➤ Academy Award Nominations are announced this
month.

COLD & FLU EXCUSES

With the cold and flu season in full force, medical problems
become even more bizarre when you ask your listeners.
Samples taken from actual student notes:

➤ Please excuse Bobby from school yesterday, he had
a stomach egg!
➤ Stanley had to miss some school. He had an attack
of whooping cranes in his chest.
➤ Please excuse Connie from gym class today as she
had difficulty breeding!

*Try to get involved in a Snow Sculpture
Contest...this has been increasingly popular in recent
years. In fact there is now a national organization
that coordinates snow sculptors.*

Phone

Numbers For Feb 2:
Punxsutawney Mayor's Office 814 938-2710
WPXZ Radio/Punxsutawney   814 938-6000
Punxsutawney Cake & Steak 814 938-8191

GROUND HOG DAY

S ome parts of the country will do more with this than others. Here are some ideas:

➤ Record messages from the ground hog...speed up your voice chipmunk-style.

➤ Send someone to Punxsutawney, Pa. for the ceremony.

➤ Sponsor a Groundhog Run...10K race...donate proceeds to charity.

➤ Have the morning show act as the groundhog, and bury them somewhere in the city, broadcasting that the groundhog will emerge at a specific time. They are the groundhog when they pop up through a ground hog.

➤ Try a Ground Hog parade down a city street.

➤ Give away "gound hog"...pork sausage

Don't forget to get those drops from the movie "Ground Hog Day" starring Bill Murray....there's some great material.

"How Cold Is It"?

Here's a quick anf fun bit that could turn into a phone topic for you, too. As you know, February is one of the coldest months of the year1

- ➢ If it's 50 degrees, New York tenants turn on the heat, Wisconsinites plant gardens.
- ➢ If it's 40 degrees, Californians shiver uncontrollably, Canadians sunbathe.
- ➢ If it's 35 degrees, Italian cars don't start.
- ➢ If it's 32 degrees, distilled water freezes.
- ➢ If it's 30 degrees, you can see your breath, you plan a vacation to Florida, politicians begin to worry about the homeless, Wisconsinites eat ice cream.
- ➢ If it's 25 degrees, Boston water freezes, Californians weep pitably, the cat insists on sleeping on your bed with you.
- ➢ If it's 20 degrees, Cleveland water freezes, San Franciscans start thinking favorably of Los Angeles, Green Bay fans put on t-shirts.
- ➢ If it's 15 degrees, you plan a vacation in Acapulco, Wisconsinites go swimming.
- ➢ If it's 10 degrees, politicians begin to talk about the homeless, too cold to snow, you need jumper cables to get the car going.
- ➢ If it's 0 degrees, New York landlords turn on the heat, Sheboygan brats grill on the patio... yum!
- ➢ If it's 5 below, you can hear your breath, you plan a vacation in Hawaii.
- ➢ If it's 10 below, American cars don't start, it's too cold to skate.

PRESIDENT'S DAY

To celebrate the birthday of Lincoln & Washington, President's Day gets everyone a day off of work, and creates some great sales at retail! PRESIDENTIAL Facts:

➤ George Washington was the third cousin twice removed of Robert E. Lee.

➤ Warren G. Harding was the first president whose father was alive when he was elected president; he is also the first president to be survived by his father.

➤ George Washington's mother did not care much for her famous son's politics. She was a Tory at heart and refused to appear at either of George's inaugurations.

➤ George Washington had size 13 feet.

➤ All U.S. Presidents have worn eyeglasses. Most removed them in public.

➤ Abe Lincoln was tall and muscular; he had a 32 inch waist and wore size 14 boots.

➤ How many U.S. presidents, are not buried in the United States? Five: Carter, Ford, Reagan, Bush and Clinton.

➤ What does the "S" in Harry S. Truman, stand for? Nothing. His parents couldn't decide on a middle name, so they just gave him the initial "S."

➤ Which president in history, was so fat, that he got stuck in a bathtub? William Howard Taft, 1909-1913 born, in the U.S. 5) And what? Answer: you must be elected.

-128-

MARCH

Here comes springtime! It's still cold in a lot of the country, but Spring begins in the middle of the month. Promotionally, set up your St. Patrick's Day plans early and don't wait too long to launch your best material for the spring ratings period.

- ➢ Spring begins this month.
- ➢ "On-Hold" month. Entice your audience to switch to your station during the month and play your signal on their phone system. Promote the switch to your station for about 10 days during which time you encourage your listeners to let you know you are now "On-Hold." Then, every day place several random calls. If you find your station on their system, they win.
- ➢ Easter Seal Telethon
- ➢ Red Cross Month

Mardi Gras in New Orleans is coming up. For Fat Tuesday call to check in on the festivities

St. Patrick's Day ideas are in the section on Holidays in this book

- ➤ National Noodle Month (listeners bobbing in spaghetti for prizes)
- ➤ Frozen Food Month
- ➤ Foot Health Month (give away some foot massages)
- ➤ National Nutrition Month.
- ➤ Talk With Your Teen About Sex Month
- ➤ National Sauce Month
- ➤ Music In Our Schools Month. Have kids call in and play their instruments on the air. Or put together a band for a morning show concert. If you want to be a hero, find a school with no funding for a music department and lead the charge!

Also this month:

- ➤ National Procrastination Week (sponsored by Procrastinators' Club of America in Bryn Athyn, Pa)
- ➤ National Panic Day (sponsored by Sky Is Falling Committee in Lancaster, Pa)
- ➤ American Chocolate Week.
- ➤ Peanut Butter Lovers' Day (have listeners call in with a mouth full of peanut butter to recite poems or sing songs

THE ACADEMY AWARDS

- ➤ Give away tickets to nominated movies
- ➤ Hold listener watching party marathon
- ➤ Giveaway copies of movies available on video
- ➤ Remember, it's not so much about who *won,* but about *what they wore!*

GRAMMY AWARDS

How a bout a "Take your Granny to the Grammies contest. If you win, you have to take your grand mother, and call in with live reports from the show. Makes for a great week or so of morning show bits.

Try to line up a live broadcast from the Grammy Awards. It's a great opportunity because ALL the stars are there. Work directly with the Grammy Awards publicity department or pull some strings with the record labels!

SPRING TRAINING

Plan to send your morning show to Spring Training if you have a local baseball team. Do their show live from the hotel lobby and interview players, coaches, fans, etc. You may even give away a prize to a winner to accompany the show for 4-5 days, and tickets to area attractions (Florida's Disney World, etc.). Try to get the morning show (and listeners) an opportunity to work out with the team one day.

National Bathroom Reading week. What is the ideal reading material in the bathroom? People Magazine is the most popular. In the movie THE BIG CHILL, there's a great drop that says all the articles in People are just long enough for one sitting.

-129-

APRIL

- ➢ Daylight Savings Time starts this month—Spring Forward, Fall Back!
- ➢ National Cherry Blossom Festival is early in April-Washington D.C.
- ➢ Chicken Little Awards are this month...awarded by National Anxiety Center each year...Contact Alan Caruba at (201) 763-6392
- ➢ Cancer Control Month
- ➢ Community Services Month
- ➢ Holy Humor Month
- ➢ Twit Award Month
- ➢ International Guitar Month
- ➢ Knuckles Down Month
- ➢ The Boston Marathon is in middle of month. J
- ➢ Big Brothers/Big Sisters Appreciation Week is this month. You might do a morning on the program, and encourage volunteers to get involved.
- ➢ National Convention of American Mothers is in Woodland Hills, Ca. They award their annual Mother Of the Year.   Also, you can select your OWN mother of the year. Have listeners call in to nominate.
- ➢ National Cable Month

EARTH DAY

➤ Happy Earthday to you. Change lyrics of songs for appropriate responses.

➤ Do the show from a recycling center, trying to get _____ pounds of recycleable trash during the show.   Listeners come by with trash & receive free donuts and coffee.

➤ Recycle the morning personalities. They do their show from *inside* the recycling containers, with listeners bringing in their stuff to cover the show.

➤ "Garbage-fest". It's a big party that focuses on cleaning up the town/area. Have local or national bands in to play.

➤ Tree Shirts...Have your station logo designed into a Tree and give away TREE SHIRTS.

➤ Plant trees in a park in your listeners names.

April Fool ideas are in the section on Holidays in this book

BASEBALL SEASON

Opening Day is usually in early April (sometimes in late March). Here's a Special Season Opening Baseball Quiz:

1. What is the maximum number of participants that can be on the field directly involved in the play at one time? Count umpires and coaches but not managers or bullpen players. (20. 9 defensive players, four umpires, two coaches, three on base, one at bat, one on deck.)

2. A pitcher faces 27 batters and strikes them all out, yet his team loses 6-0. How is this possible? (He was brought in as a relief pitcher after six runs scored in the first inning.)

3. How many hits in one inning can a team get and yet not score any runs? (Six. Three singles followed by three runners hit by batted balls; the runner is out, but the batter is credited with a single.)

4. Walter Johnson, Bob Gibson, and Don Drysdale have all thrown four strikeouts in one inning. Explain. (If a catcher drops the third strike and fails to throw the batter out at first, the man is safe.)

5. During a nine-inning game, the Mighty Casey came to bat nine times, once in each inning. What is the fewest number of runs that Casey's team could have scored in the game? (No runs. Casey bats first in the lineup, and in the first inning, he and the next two batters walk, and the next three strike out. In the second inning, the first three men

walk, bringing Casey to bat again, but the three base runners are each caught off base by the pitcher which brings Casey to bat again at the top of the third inning. This cycle repeats until the game ends.)

6. There are six ways a batter can reach first base safely without getting a hit. A walk is one. How many others an you name? (Error; hit by pitch; catcher drops third strike; catcher's interference; fielder's choice.)

7. Willie Mays hit more home runs in the first inning than in any other inning. Some theorize it was because Mays got tired as games went on. The real reason is simpler. What is it? (Mays always batted third in the lineup, so he always came to bat at least once in every first inning.)

8. In one baseball game, The Rockets beat the Fliers 9-0, yet no man ever crossed second base. There are two possible answers. (1: The Rockets and Fliers are women's teams. 2: The Fliers forfeit the game. When a game is forfeited, the rules state the score shall be recorded as 9-0.)

9. Name four terms used in both baseball and music. (Here are five: pitch, score, run, slide, and tie.)

10. Name seven terms used in both baseball and bridge. (Here are 11: diamond, club, ace, rubber, grand slam, deck, signals, lead, steal, double, sacrifice.)

From The Desk Of...Tom Boswell

"Life begins on Opening Day."

-130-

MAY

The calendar may say Spring, but the audience is FEELING Summer. Kids are anxious for school to end, and everyone wants to be outside! Get out there with them!

- ➤ National Barbecue Month. Giveaways can include grills, steaks, hamburger, hot dogs, charcoal, aprons, chef hats, etc. How about putting together a package for one winner to entertain 20 of their friends in a backyard barbecue at their home? Bring all of the barbecue equipment, and leave it with the winner as a prize.
- ➤ American Bike Month.
- ➤ Correct Posture Month. Sponsored by American Chiropractic Assn.
- ➤ Eat What You Want Day. Sponsored by the Wellness Permission League, headed by Thomas Roy. He says that for one day a year, you should eat whatever you want, even if it's bad for you. Call Mr. Roy at (717) 866-5193.
- ➤ Limerick Day. Use your imagination!
- ➤ National Third Shift Workers Day. A good bit for overnighters. Do a co-promotion with all night businesses.
- ➤ National Memo Day is this month (usually around

May 21). It's a day set aside to call attention to unneeded memos handed down from management. Tie in a local restaurant, and give away lunch to the office that calls in with the stupidest office memo.

➤ PTA Teacher Appreciation Week
➤ The National Spelling Bee finals are in Washington DC toward the end of the month. Getting kids on the air that are great spellers can be entertaining.
➤ The Children's Miracle Network Telethon is this month, a big money-raising event for children's hospitals across America. Contact your local office and volunteer your station's support. Try to get the morning show on as one of the anchors.

This is a big month for the biggest movies and TV season finales! Now is the time to contact:

a) the big movie distributors (Fox, Paramount, Universal, etc.)   b) the distributor's ad agency (distributor will tell you who it is for your region);
c) the exhibitor (owner of theater chain that has bought the right to show the film in your market).

For television, May (and November) are the biggest months of the year. Season finales and cliffhangers are scheduled to coincide with this important ratings month. It's usually the easiest time to get an interview with a celebrity on TV, and a great month to work with your local network affiliates for cross promotion. If you are looking to get some free visibility on TV, May is your best chance!

NATIONAL PET WEEK

➤ Stupid Pet Tricks. Listeners bring pets and compete with this Letterman-like contest for prizes. Hold it at a mall or pet shop.

➤ Do PSA features for Humane Society. Each day, the society can bring in an animal and you find someone to adopt it.

➤ Barking for Bucks. Pay listeners a dollar for each time they get their dog to bark in 30 seconds.

➤ Phone bit: If you were told your pet was sick and needed an operation, but it would cost $5,000...would you pay for it or let your dog die? By the way, it is a fact that they have braces for dogs now...not to mention bone marrow transplants.

Things You'll Never Hear At A NASCAR Race:

Now explain this to me again... they just go around in circles?

Isn't that Hillary Clinton sitting over there?

Taladega? Is that some kind of Mexican food?

I wish they would start selling some health food at this track.

I hope I get home in time tonight for "Jeopardy."

Oops, gotta run. Gotta get back to my job at the jet propulsion lab.

Excuse me, do have any Grey Poupon?

The hell with the boys in the garage and pits... it was my superior driving ability!

Memorial Day ideas are in the section on Holidays

Sports

Not only is baseball in full swing, but **The Kentucky Derby** and **Indianapolis 500** take place this month.

The Derby is called the most exciting two minutes in sports. It's followed by the Preakness and Belmont Stakes in the pursuit for Horse Racing's Triple Crown.

The **Indianapolis 500** usually brings out some station promotions:

> ➤ Hold the UNDY 500. Listeners race wearing only their underwear-or wearing underwear on their heads.

> ➤ Indiana Jones 500. Giveaway 500 tickets to a screening of all 3 Indiana Jones movies (or copy of video cassette of all 3). Sell it as 500 minutes of Indy Jones.

> ➤ Hold an ELECTRONIC 500...battery powered or remote controlled vehicle races held at public location. Should be a big family event, and is usually good for TV coverage.

Cinco De Mayo

This Mexican holiday is May 5 (their Independence Day-equivalent of 4th of July in USA). The fifth of May is the day on which Mexicans and Mexican-Americans commemorate the defeat of the French. It is a national Holiday second in importance only to September 16, Independence Day. Even as early as 1863, the day was celebrated by Mexican speeches, songs and parades.

- ➤ Mexican Millionaire-give away a million pesos (usually under $500 cash, depending on the exchange rate).
- ➤ Club Night-Listeners come dressed in Mexican outfits, have mexican activities (Jalapeno eating contest, hat dance, taco tossing contest, etc). Lots of free Mexican food, of course.
- ➤ If a MIX station, tie into the MIXICAN holiday.
- ➤ Play bilingual (Spanish) versions of hits in your library.
- ➤ Bring a mariachi band into the morning show
- ➤ Give away packs of Mexican items all day long.
- ➤ Grand Salsa Dip: Listeners dive into a giant vat of salsa and dig around for prizes (pesos).
- ➤ Human Pinata-Morning show wears velcro suit with prizes attached. Listeners knock off the prizes with a foam rubber bat...keep the prizes they knock off.

- ➢ Sink full of Mayo....fill a sink and have listeners reach in for prizes.
- ➢ Make the "World's Largest Margarita"

-131-

JUNE

I t's a great month. School gets out, summer is starting and life is exploding all around you. Plan now to take advantage of those weddings, graduations and other events in you audience's lives. It's also one of the most important ratings months in the year at most radio stations.

June is:

- ➢ Adopt-a-cat month. Good chance to have a warm and fuzzy morning personality find a home for a cat each morning. Work with humane society. Try to provide a month of kitty litter and cat food for each.
- ➢ National Dairy Month. Arrange for a competitive milk-off. Work it out with a farmer who has cows, and bring three listeners in to see who can get the most milk in 30 seconds.
- ➢ Accordian Awareness Month. Accordians are funny. Try to find someone who can play it for your morning show. Check with local polka bands.
- ➢ This is National Drive Safe Month...shouldn't EVERY month be so named? Create a male/female

competition in your parking lot to determine who are better drivers-male or female. Get a state driving test administrator to judge.

➢ National Zoo and Aquarium Month. Find out about it and be visible at the event. Some zoos will offer free admission one day in June.
➢ Flag Day
➢ National Donut Day
➢ Belmont Stakes at Belmont Park in New York (third jewel in horse racing's triple crown).
➢ County fairs and festivals. Give away cotton candy, popcorn, etc. with your call letters on them. Have your morning show buried alive or frozen alive at your booth. Call the infamous Dr. Silkini for details.

National Ice Cream day is July 16. Have listeners dive into ice cream for prizes, create world's largest ice cream sundae or
give away ice cream cones on the street at lunch

June is also the perfect time to make regular visits to area beaches and pools, handing out prizes.

The first Day of Summer and the longest day of the year occur in June. Wouldn't it be cool to send listeners to the Land of the Midnight Sun...Alaska. Nome, Alaska celebrates the Midnight Sun Festival June 20 and 21.

Announce the specific locations you will be visiting and when. Prizes can include sodas (cold, of course), station merchandise, cassettes, gift certificates, movie rental coupons, even envelopes with cash!

WEDDING MONTH!.

June is the perfect times to involve your station with wedding promotions.

➤ Americans are one and a half times more likely to be married in June than in any other month.

➤ Ancient Romans considered June the most favorable month in which to be wed, especially during a full moon or at the conjunction of the moon and sun.

➤ The Romans also customarily broke cake over the bride's head. Wedding guests then picked up the pieces for their own good luck.

➤ According to an old belief, wedding rings were placed on the fourth finger because it was thought to contain a nerve going straight to the heart.

➤ The expression "tie the knot" began with the Danes, who tied an actual knot in pieces of string or fabric

Great morning show questions

-If the woman breaks off an engagement, should she give the ring back?

-Wedding horror stories

-Brides to be call in to vent their frustrations on planning problems and visitors from hell!

Father's Day ideas are in the section on Holidays in this book

at weddings. The tradition spread to England and other parts of Europe.

➤ Women in ancient Greece counted their age from their wedding date, rather than their date of birth.

How to Give Away a Wedding

Arrange a number of wedding related businesses or sponsors (jewelry store, tux shop, bakery, caterer, travel agency, flower shop, etc.). These businesses give away a complete wedding, which you will broadcast on the morning show, of course.

1. First, listeners call in the wildest wedding proposals of all time. It doesn't have to be ones that have happened to them, just proposals they know of. You'll have calls telling you about renting a gorilla suit, a knight riding up on a horse, etc.

2. Next, take the best stories and get the details straight so you can recreate them. In other words, rent the gorilla suit, find a white horse to ride up on, etc.

3. Now, find three guys who are really ready to propose, and play their promise to propose on the morning show.

4. Finally, bring the newly engaged couples into your studio to play the Newly-Engaged Game...just like the Newlywed Game. Ask questions like, "If your love life were an all-you-can-eat Mexican buffet, would if be hot and spicy or fast-food?" This is a great opportunity to create theater of the mind, and build the bit into something BIG-

GRADUATION

D on't miss the perfect opportunity to generate revenue through clients and relaate to your listeners. Include graduates from high school, college and even elementary/junior high schools.

Prizes you can give away:
-Catering from a local restaurant
-Party supplies (balloons, etc.) from a local party store
-Sound system with one of your jocks

How to give it away:

➢ Parents call in to tell stories about what makes their grad so special. The best story wins.

➢ Bring three graduating students into the studio to play the GRADUATION GAME. Each student brings one of their parents and you play a Newlywed-game style contest. Sample questions:
What's the most trouble you've ever gotten into?
Who did you have your first crush on?
What subject does your graduate have the most problem with?

➢ Another morning show bit idea: Biggest cliches used in commencement speeches. This is pretty funny. Take the best ones and enter people that called them in into a drawing for the graduation party package.

-132-

JULY

Finally, summer is here, and the heat is ON. Listeners are on vacation, the 4th of July brings out our patriotic spirit and everyone is focused on FUN!

National Hot Dog Month. Here are some facts:

The average person eats about 60 per year.

The longest was a 1,983 foot weiner made by Bil-Mar Foods of Zeeland, Michigan, in 1983.

20 million will be eaten at baseball stadiums this season.

The record for most sold in a year is 2.3 million, at Denver's Mile High Stadium, breaking the previous record of 1.5 million at O'Hare Airport in Chicago.

Nathan's Coney Island in Brooklyn, NY has an annual hot dog eating contest., Recently, the winner consumed 19 and a half dogs in 12 minutes.

- ➢ National Baked Bean Month
- ➢ National Ice Cream Month.
- ➢ National Picnic Month
- ➢ Anti-Boredom Month...call the Boring Institute
- ➢ Hitchhiking Month.
- ➢ National NUDITY Days are in July. Your morning show will have fun by inviting nudists in to do your

July 4 and Summer ideas are in the section on Holidays in this book

morning show.

Since the Major League All Star game is in July, here's a great trivia question. "There are only three days each year that none of the four major sports leagues play games (NHL, NBA, NFL, Major League Baseball). What are they?" The three days of the baseball All-Star break.

This month marks the 1/2 way point of the year (July 1)...182 days have elapsed, with 183 remaining.

The official DOG DAYS of summer are July 3 through August 15. The hottest days of the year in the northern hemisphere earned its' name through a legend that says "dogs grew mad".

This is a bad month for allergies .. and a good time to solicit calls for allergy stories.

-133-

AUGUST

A ugust is the toughest month in radio. Everyone is on vacation, phones are dead, listeners are bored, and parents can't wait for school to start. The best advice is to take vacation yourself and re-energize your attitude for the upcoming fall book!

➤ Psychic week is early in August. Have a Palm Reader in the studio. Listeners fax in their palms and have them read. Solicit weird psychic encounter stories. Talk to local police about using a psychic to solve a crime

➤ National Smile Week is this month...send an intern to normally depressing places (morgue, hospital, etc.) with a smile. Or for a real warm and fuzzy, send your jocks to Children's Hospitals with toys and prizes.

➤ National Catfish Month...How about BOBBING FOR CATFISH. Hey, I *told* you this month was tough!

➤ It's Romance Awareness Month...to encourage couples to display romance on other days besides Valentine's Day.

This is a great month to line up a charity promotion with your local minor league baseball (or college football) team.

Use local TV personalities, columnists, and of course your airstaff. You can even set up a contest to see who gets the most "tips".

-134-

SEPTEMBER

➤ Baby Safety Month - Sponsored by the Juvenile Products Manufacturers Assn.
➤ Be Kind To Editors And Writers Month
➤ International Gay Square Dance Month - No joke! Sponsored by the International Association of Gay Square Dancers.
➤ National Bed Check Month - To remind people to check your mattress for wear and tear. There's no end to the bits you can do with this one. Call people and wake them up, telling them it's National Bed Check Month and that you're from the Better Sleep Council and if they could go check their mattress for wear and tear.
➤ National Chicken Month
➤ Self Improvement Month
➤ National Courtesy Month: to celebrate the benefit of mutual love and respect. Have your talent become COURTESY COPS to ticket people for rude behavior (listeners calling, etc.). Have an etiquette expert test listeners on their manners...only accept polite requests on the air.
➤ National Honey Month
➤ Pleasure Your Mate Month: Give away romantic weekends, gift certificates to Victoria's Secret, etc. Phone bit: What signals do you have to let your mate know you are "in the mood"

In America, Sept. 11, 2001 is the day that changed life as we know it. It's the day of the terrorist attacks on the World Trade Center.

Labor Day And End-Of-Summer ideas are in the section on Holidays in this book

-135-

OCTOBER

October's cooler temperatures and changing seasons brings another mood change. Halloween gets bigger every year, and football shares center stage with baseball!

- ➤ Adopt-a-shelter-dog month
- ➤ Auto Battery Safety month
- ➤ Campaign for healthier babies month
- ➤ Computer learning month
- ➤ Consumer Information month
- ➤ Co-op awareness month
- ➤ Energy awareness month
- ➤ Family History month
- ➤ Cookbook month
- ➤ Lupus awareness month
- ➤ National AIDS awareness month
- ➤ National Apple Jack month
- ➤ National Book Fair month
- ➤ National Dental Hygeine month
- ➤ National Depression Education and Awareness month
- ➤ National Dessert month
- ➤ National Disability Employment Awareness month
- ➤ National Family Sexuality Education month
- ➤ National Kitchen and Bath month
- ➤ National liver awareness month
- ➤ National Pasta month

Halloween ideas are in the section on Holidays in this book

- ➤ National Pizza month
- ➤ National Popcorn Poppin' month
- ➤ National Sarcastics awareness month
- ➤ National Youth against Tobacco month

COLUMBUS DAY

Columbus discovered the new world, not be confused with the Old World, The Third World, or Disney World. Of course Columbus thought the "New World" was India.

He didn't know where he was going or where he was when he got there. He discovered America, which he named El Salvador, thinking it was China when it was actually the Bahamas. Let's face it. Columbus was so lost he'd have been happy to discover the Bermuda Triangle.

Columbus was gone so long he was officially listed as a missing person.

Talk about hardship. Chris took 70 days to sail from Europe to the "New World."

500 years ago his cruise ships were called the Nina, Pinta and Santa Maria.

NOTE: If you have the disc and format allows "Stan Freberg Presents The United States Of America" on Capitol has a terrific "Columbus Discovers America" routine done in the style of a Broadway musical. There's lots of other "Holiday" type material on it for Thanksgiving, Paul Revere, Ben Franklin discovers Electricity and Fourth of July.

-136-

NOVEMBER

As Halloween fades and November begins, your audience turns their attentions to "the Holidays". Thanksgiving is a preamble to Christmas, and increasingly, audience's attentions become more and more difficult to harness.

> ➤ National Children's Book Week. It encourages the enjoyment of reading. Get moms and dads to put their kids on the phone to read a few pages of their favorite books. A 7 year old reading "Cat In the Hat" is great radio.

Election Day

Have people bring by old campaign signs to help clean up the leftover trash. Whoever brings the most signs wins cash.

How about mud slinging on Election Day? Send your producer to a high traffic polling location. Listeners come by and sling mud at him on the air. Bring a box of latex gloves so listeners can practice "safe slinging."

Go to an elementary school with a tape deck…ask kids what they would do if they were president (or governor, or mayor).

Thanksgiving ideas are in the section on Holidays in this book

GREAT AMERICAN SMOKE OUT

The Smokeout is held each year on the third Thursday in November.

➤ Work with the American Lung Assn to get an old cigarette vending machine and have people take hacks at it with a sledgehammer. In exchange, you give smokers a BEAT THE HABIT survival kit, including literature on smoking nicotine gum and candy.

➤ How about a SMOKEOUT luncheon at a local restaurant.

➤ Adopt-A-Smoker. Get a listener willing to quit smoking for the day. Then through out the morning and afternoon you will call him/her to check up on them. Tell them you will do anything in your powers to help them stay sane.

➤ Get a nonsmoker to wear a nicotine patch during your show and tell you what it feels like.

➤ Best smoker's cough. Have 'em call it in and hack it up.

➤ Times when you really NEED a cigarette: after a big meal, with your first cup of coffee, after sex, whenever your in-laws come to visit, before giving a speech, any time you're having a drink in a bar, as soon as you get out of an important meeting, or whenever you're talking on the phone for a long time.

-137-

December

The Holiday Season is here, and promotionally, that's all you need to know! Your entire month will be dominated by holiday content, but if you *must* have something else:

BINGO was invented in December, 1929. Contact Bingo expert Roger Snowden at 800 327-6437 for more information, but you could hold special bingo games at client locations this month...

And, of course December 7, 1941 is the day that will live in infamy...Pearl Harbor Day.

CREDITS

Seth Swirsky: The book *Every Pitcher Tells A Story* is a great read for any baseball fan. The story about Jim Rooker walking from Philadelphia to Pittsburgh came from Seth's book.

ESP Media, Australia. This International consulting firm is constantly re-inventing the way their clients approach personality radio in Australia, Asia and Europe. Their methods of evaluating and critiquing talent are outstanding.

Alex DeMers, Demers Programming. (610) 363-2636. Alex & Company provide outstanding programming advice and produce a thoughtful newsletter for programmers, with valuable input for talent.

Elizabeth Burley Bruce-Larry Bruce Communications

Morning Mouth Magazine (770) 926-7573. By far the finest publication directed to air talent, *Morning Mouth* is a must-read for serious talent.

Randy Lane, the Randy Lane Company. Randy is one of the world's finest talent coaches. As a former programmer, he understands the programming aspects of morning shows with a sensitivity to the needs and desires of talent. His "20 Areas of Evaluation" (Morning Radio 1) is an ideal standard for measuring a show.

Page Nienaber, Clifton Radio. Page is a promotion genius. From stunting to contestinig to public appearances, Page delivers! His articles and advice have inspired several ideas in this book, and reminded me of many others.

Albie Dee. One of the finest, most creative air personalities ever, Albie's work is reflected in this book several times.

Alan Burns, Alan Burns & Associates (703) 648-0000. Alan is one of my most influential mentors, and is personally responsible for teaching me the basics of creating great radio stations. The co-author of *Morning Radio,* Alan continues strong as a world class consultant.

Walt Sabo, Sabo Media (212) 808-3005. The originator of FM Hot Talk, Walt's strength is his ability to work with talent to appeal to an audience on an emotional level. He thinks with a listener's perspective-a strength that all programmers could use. Walt's work provided inspiration and ideas throughout this book.

Radio Ink Magazine. A leading trade publication for management, their articles and coverage of personalities provided background and information for some of the insight in several sections.

Phil Hendrie, Premeire Radio Networks. A personal favorite, Phil does radio like nobody else!

Kid Kraddick, Premeire Radio Networks. From the examples in the book, you can easily detect my admiration for Kid's work.

Steve Reynolds, Talent Coach. As a programmer and talent, Steve knows how to put it all together and does just that with many morning shows and groups.

Pat Welsh, Pollack Media (310) 459-8556. Pat's straight-forward, logical approach to programming is reflected in the articles he writes. Not only do I agree with most of what Pat presents, I've found much useful information in his work.

Mark Ramsey, Nova Marketing Group Inc. (858) 490-8881. Mark's brilliant article about creating "story arcs" is reprinted with his permission in this book. Thanks, Mark!

Alan Mason, Audience Development Group. Working with management, Alan is able to bridge the gap between programming principles and sales interests. He has keen insight in applying real-life examples to radio marketing situations. Many of those examples have been adapted in *Morning Radio 2*.

Dave Ryan, KDWM/Minneapolis. Dave is a premeire talent, and published author in *Morning Mouth*. I've used many of his thoughts representing the point of view of the announcer.

Airplay Monitor Magazine (800) 745-8922. A great source of promotional ideas, I found several examples of stunts and contests to demonstrate the principles explored in the book.

Secret Formulas of The Wizard Of Ads-Roy Williams. Everyone in the radio industry should get Roy's books. The ideas, thought process and examples can be adapted to all aspects of the business. I've learned much from his publications, and you'll notice the similarity in our philosophies in many places.

Todd Wallace, Consultant *(480) 443-3500.* Legendary programmer and consultant Todd Wallace publishes a monthly programming newsletter called *Programmer's Digest.* It's loaded with ideas, insight and examples. The publication was an invaluable resource in compiling examples for the book.

The Road to Optimism-Dr. J. Mitchell Perry. To win in radio, you must think positively. Dr. Perry's book helps you learn to not only do that, but portray it in your every day life. Several of his ideas have been adapted to the radio in this book.

Wooden: A Lifetime of Observations and Reflections On and Off the Court-Coach John Wooden with Steve Jamison
In The Zone-Dr. J. Mitchell Perry and Steve Jamison. Coaching air talent and athletes are very similar. These books are loaded with examples, many of which are used in *Morning Radio.*

Michelle Stevens, Sr. VP/Programming, Nassau Broadcasting. Michelle is responsible for dozens of successful personalities, and her thoughts on "Leveraging Emotions" is a highlight of this book.

John Coleman, Coleman Research. Coleman conducts some of the most reliable and innovative research in radio. Many of the principles I've come to discover have been inspired by, or confirmed by, John's work.

www.lured.com is a terrific resource f or promotion ideas, contest ideas and worksheets. Several concepts provided inspiration for content in this book.

Morning Radio

In 1999, the book **Morning Radio** **was released, and rapidly became accepted as a powerful, step-by-step guide for air personalities, programmers and managers. In a short time, it became a textbook for hundreds of air personalities worldwide to help on their journey to winning radio! Authored by** <u>Tracy Johnson and Alan Burns</u>**, Morning Radio is one of the most powerful tools to make your show stand out! It's loaded with examples and real-life stories from some of the world's best air personalities.**

Now, the second book in the series takes those principles one step further. *Morning Radio II: Turning the Science into Art* **offers useful, practical applications to turn your content into actionable material on the air.**

To order *Morning Radio: A Guide to Developing On Air Superstars*, visit <u>www.tjohnsonmedia.com</u>.

Comments about *Morning Radio: A Guide to Developing On Air Superstars*

This is the best book I've ever read on radio-period! Whether you're a Program Director, and On-Air Personality or a General Manager, GET IT AND READ IT"
Scott Shannon, WPLJ/New York

"I don't care what it takes...if you're serious about your career, you've got to get this book!"
Jeff & Jer, Star 100.7/San Diego

"A clear, concise, step-by-step blueprint for building a successful morning show, managing the people who do it and making them happy while they do it. "Wanna win? Read this book"
Sean Phillips, PD KHTT/Tulsa

Forget Stanford, forget Princeton, everything you need to learn about hosting or developing a great morning show is right here."
Tony Novia
Contemporary Hit Radio Editor
Radio & Records Newspaper

A must read for program director's working with growing morning shows, as well as each member of the show
Greg Strassell, PD, WBMX/Boston

Morning Radio is the primary volume in an all-too-thin programming library. Thanks for everything!
Tim Richards, WKQI/Detroit

There is a dynamic new book "MORNING RADIO," authored by ALAN BURNS& ASSOCIATES President ALAN BURNS and KFMB-A&F/SAN DIEGO GM TRACY JOHNSON.
Joel Denver-All Access

Order Form

Order additional copies of *Morning Radio II: Turning Science into Art,* or place an order for *Morning Radio I: A Guide to Developing On-Air Superstars.*

__ **Please send _____ copies of *Morning Radio II: Turning Science into Art*   U.S. $54.95, includes shipping!**

__ **Please send _____ copies of *Morning Radio I: A Guide to Developing On-Air Superstars*   U.S. $69.95, includes shipping!**

Name _____

Company _____

Address _____

City _____ State _____ Zip _____

Country _____ Telephone _____

E-mail address _____

Payment:
All payment must be in U.S. funds only. Discounts are available for purchases of 10 copies or more, and educational institutions. Call or email tjohnson@kfmb.com for details.

Credit Card Number _____ Exp._____

Name on Card _____

Total Amount _____

Phone orders: 858 232-2897
Order online at www.tjohnsonmedia.com

Tracy Johnson is General Manager
of KFMB AM & FM (Star 100.7) in San Diego. He has
been recognized as one of America's leading programmers by broadcasting industry organizations
such as Billboard, Gavin, Radio & Records, Network
40 and more. In 1998, Johnson was honored as "Best
Programmer in America" in a poll of industry experts in
Radio Ink magazine.

Johnson's programming accomplishments have been
achieved by recruiting, developing, showcasing and
establishing a "partnership" for success with top air
talent. His unique perspective and skills in recognizing and managing talent has been the single most
important ingredient in his impressive track record.

www.tjohnsonmedia.com